Caribbean Elegance

Caribbean Elegance

MICHAEL CONNORS

PHOTOGRAPHS BY BRUCE BUCK

HARRY N. ABRAMS, INC., PUBLISHERS

Contents

Page 2:
A typical colonial seating
arrangement on the French
island of Martinique

opposite:
A Caribbean shell collection,
Martinique

Preface

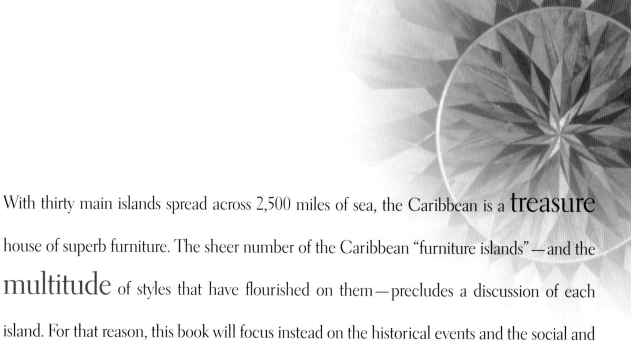

With thirty main islands spread across 2,500 miles of sea, the Caribbean is a treasure house of superb furniture. The sheer number of the Caribbean "furniture islands"—and the multitude of styles that have flourished on them—precludes a discussion of each island. For that reason, this book will focus instead on the historical events and the social and economic factors that have contributed to the development of the forms unique to Caribbean furniture design.

Although the region's heritage dates back more than 3,000 years, the development of West Indian furniture did not really begin until the eighteenth century. Over the course of the subsequent 300 years, the European styles of the colonizing nations of Spain, England, Holland, Denmark, and France influenced furniture design in the Caribbean. To these multi-faceted influences were added those of Africa and North America, as well as manifestations of the region's history of slavery.

Introduction

The West Indies have long lured the adventurous and the romantic to their shores. The islands' promise of new freedoms and unimagined excesses exuded a compelling magic. Unbounded by territory, unrestrained by a continent's conventionality, the West Indies are floating lands of the languid and the lavish bordered by beaches and guided by the rhythms of the seas. Moreover, the islands of the West Indies exist enticingly as the linking chain between North and South America. The Caribbean Sea and the Atlantic Ocean surround them and the trade winds glide gently over their vistas. Colonizing nations, adventurers, pirates, and plunderers were attracted to the West Indies by the wealth of possibilities and the possibilities of wealth.

The indigenous West Indians lived a simple and sun-drenched existence as they drifted about the archipelago in elaborately carved dugout canoes. The lives of the

Pre-Columbian Arawaks and Caribs have been studied extensively by both historians and anthropologists. The difference in temperament between the hunter-gatherer Arawaks and the fierce Caribs mirrored the difference between the normally gentle ambiance of the islands and the periodic hurricanes and volcanic eruptions that struck with ferocity. The West Indies have always been islands of extremes: the extreme divergence of temperament between the two native tribes, the extremes of the tropical weather, and later, during colonial rule, the extreme discrepancy in lifestyle between the plantocracy and the enslaved.

Although the sun continued to rise and set and the hurricanes continued to ravage, once the bold and greedy nations of Europe began colonizing the islands, the archipelago would never return to the natives' original tempo. The countries of Spain, England, Denmark, Holland, and France participated in a real-life version of "capture the flag" as they vied for control of the islands' agricultural abundance. Initially, the main crops were tobacco and cotton; later, the major resource was sugar, referred to colloquially as "white gold." "It was to these 'adventurers in trade or service'—the planters, merchants, agents or managers of plantations, colonial governors and their staffs, and other officials, together with their families, all those, that is, who made the phrase 'as rich as a West Indian' an eighteenth-century proverb—that the furniture was supplied."[1] As trade developed, so too did the demands for gracious living. To accomplish the lavish appearance of a mimicked or imagined European lifestyle, the new plantocracy at first imported fine European and North American furniture. The heat, humidity, and ravenous termites of the islands, however, soon decimated these softwood furnishings, and the planters charged local craftsmen with the task of duplicating the imported pieces using the islands' indigenous hardwoods. As time went on, the copies of the imported pieces became progressively less exact and increasingly more interpretive.

The West Indian craftsmen, most of whom were African slaves or descendants of African slaves, altered the European styles by creating the wonderfully rich and distinctive motifs of West Indian furniture: twist-and-ring designs, stylized carved palm fronds, pineapples, banana leaves, sandbox and nutmeg fruits, and zoomorphic forms. The craftsmen's interpretations thus developed an original Caribbean style that varied according to the islands' dominion and the skill of the artisan. Specifically, the individual islands developed their own colonial styles that generally incorporated the designs of furniture imported from the ruling country. On Barbados, Antigua, Jamaica, Nevis, and Saint Christopher, the English style prevailed; the French style dominated on Guadeloupe, Martinique, and Haiti; and the Spanish retained their influence over Cuba, Puerto Rico, and Hispaniola. The Dutch style dominated the "ABC" islands—Aruba, Bonaire, and Curaçao—as well as Saint Eustatius, Saba, and Saint Maarten, known as the "3-S Group." The styles of Saint Thomas, Saint John, and Saint Croix were influenced primarily by Danish furniture. Islands that changed possession with great frequency, such as Grenada and Saint Lucia, developed highly mixed styles.

Colonial West Indian furniture is the aggregation of the talents of the different islands' many craftsmen. Forms common to all islands—four-poster beds, caned mahogany rockers, settees, daybeds, and planter's chairs—exemplify the craftsmen's ability to combine form with function long before the demands of life in the twentieth century made functionality a requisite. Most West Indian design was a blend of the quintessence of imported European and North American styles and the vernacular Caribbean design. The result is a distinctive West Indian furniture whose vigorous lines bespeak a subtle opulence and casual elegance.

Part 1

THE SETTLEMENT OF THE ISLANDS

Between the Caribbean Sea, which covers an area of almost 750,000 square miles, and the Atlantic Ocean lie the West Indian islands. Like a long beckoning arm, the West Indies sweep from the shoulder of South America to the tip of Florida, linking the two continents.

The islands are, in fact, a combination of submerged volcanic peaks and ancient limestone-core and fossilized coral. These volcanic and coral islands lie in the tropics between ten degrees latitude north and the Tropic of Cancer (just twenty-three degrees latitude north). At the north end of this island chain are the four largest islands that make up the Greater Antilles: Cuba, Jamaica, Hispaniola (comprising both Haiti—or Saint-Domingue, as it was called until its formal independence in 1804—and the Dominican Republic), and Puerto Rico. To the south, stretching from Puerto Rico to the coast of Venezuela are the Lesser Antilles. The Lesser Antilles include both the Leeward Islands in the north and the Windward Islands in the south. The Leeward Islands span over 200 miles and include fifteen major islands. They extend from Anguilla and Saint Martin in the north to Dominica in the south. The Windward Islands include the island of Martinique in the north and Trinidad and Tobago in the south.

The West Indian islands vary from low coastal plains with sandy beaches to hills and mountains with deep valleys and dense rain forests. Typically, the tropical climate ranges in

fig. 1. The Petit Piton on Saint Lucia, Bay of Soufriere

temperature from seventy-six to ninety degrees Fahrenheit year round. August is the warmest month and February the coolest. Trade winds blow most of the year and destructive hurricanes are common, occasionally devastating islands during hurricane season, which occurs from the end of July through October.

The American statesman Alexander Hamilton—born on the island of Nevis—was living on Saint Croix in 1772 when a tremendous hurricane struck the island. He described the storm in a letter to his father:

> *St. Croix, September, 1772*
>
> *Honored Sir,*
>
> *I took up my pen, just to give you an imperfect account of one of the most dreadful hurricanes that memory or any records whatever can trace, which happened here on the 31ˢᵗ ultimo at night. It began about dusk, at north, and raged very violently till ten o'clock.—Then ensued a sudden and unexpected interval, which lasted about an hour. Meanwhile, the wind was shifting round to the south west point, from whence it returned with redoubled fury and continued till nearly three in the morning. Good God! What horror and destruction—it is impossible for me to describe—or you to form any idea of it. It seems as if a total dissolution of nature was taking place. The roaring of the sea and wind—fiery meteors flying about in the air—the prodigious glare of almost perpetual lightning—the crash of falling houses—and the ear-piercing shrieks of the distressed, were sufficient to strike astonishment into Angels. A great part of the buildings throughout the island are levelled to the ground— almost all the rest very much shattered—several persons killed and numbers utterly ruined—whole families roaming about the streets, unknowing where to find a place of shelter—the sick exposed to the keenness of water and air— without a bed to lie upon—or a dry covering to their bodies—and our harbors entirely bare. In a word, misery in its most hideous shapes, spread over the whole face of the country.²*

2

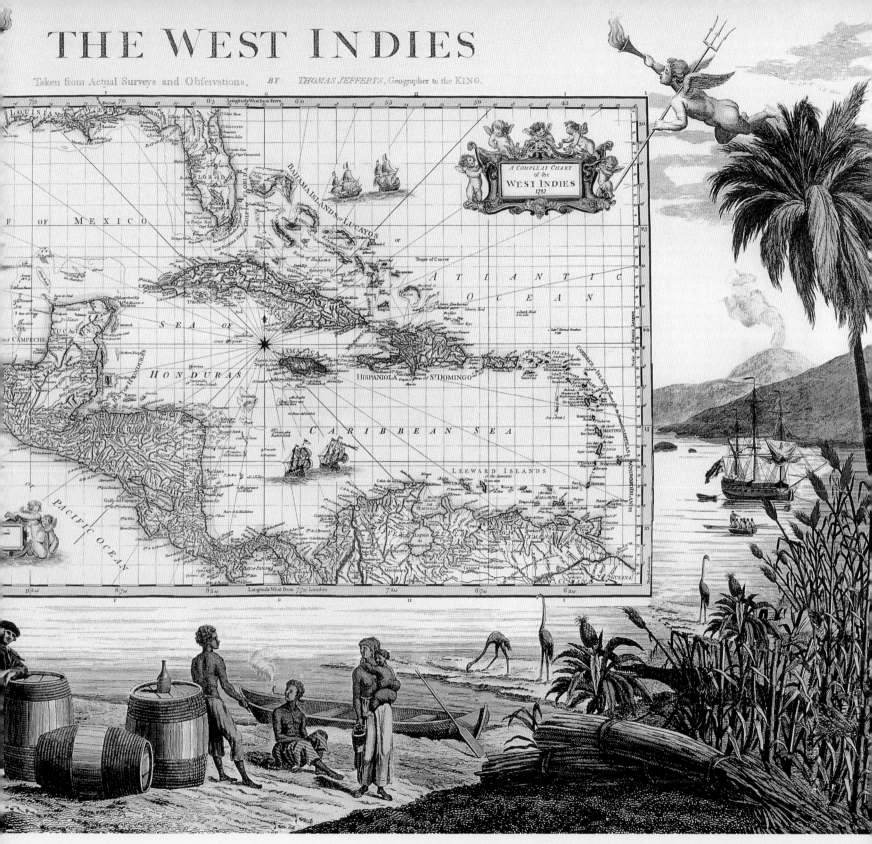

fig. 2. *A seventeenth-century map of the Caribbean*

fig. 3. A typical
Caribbean sand beach

Though the islands have a predominantly sunny and dry climate, the hurricane season coincides with the rainy months, and often brings precipitation for weeks on end. Along with the humid climate and tropical insects, hurricanes have been among the most destructive forces to the islands' colonial furniture.

For centuries Amerindians inhabited the islands. The earliest tribe, the Siboney Indians, arrived some 3,000 years ago from South America's Amazon basin. Later, the peaceful Arawak Indians slumbered beneath a benevolent sun until, about a century before the arrival of Columbus, the fierce, war-like, cannibalistic Caribs invaded. The Caribs, who gave their name to the region ("Caniba," an old spelling of "Carib," became the root of the word "cannibal," while "Carib" evolved into "Caribbean"), swept up from the jungles of Brazil and drove the Arawaks north in their effort to escape slaughter at the hands of the invaders. The Caribs' cannibalism provided an obvious pretext for enslavement by the Spanish conquistadors. Although the Caribs fervently resisted, they were ultimately exterminated under sixteenth century Spanish colonial policy, which mandated the elimination of indigenous natives throughout the Spanish territories.

The Caribbean islands began their association with the European powers in the last decade of the fifteenth century with Columbus's discovery of Cuba and Hispaniola in 1492. In 1494, Pope Alexander VI issued the Treaty of Tordesillas, which divided the New World between Spain and Portugal. Spain received all properties west of a line drawn at approximately fifty degrees longitude, which included the West Indies. Portugal received all properties to the east, which included Brazil. Each country regarded their designated territories as colonialists generally have: as resources to be exploited for the benefit of the mother country without regard for the lands' inhabitants.

Throughout the sixteenth and seventeenth centuries, the Caribbean Sea and the West Indian islands served as a battleground for the Spanish, English, French, and Dutch. Spain, which monopolized the New World wealth, stood at the fore of Catholic strength, not only in the Americas but in Europe as well. In an effort to erode Spain's European stronghold, the Protestant nations of England and Holland consistently attacked the Spanish West Indies. However, aside from random acts of pirating (each pirate group was supported financially by their nation), Spain maintained dominance on the islands for over a century.

In 1588, England finally defeated the Spanish Armada—a triumph that heralded England's prevailing sea power. Aggression against Spain escalated further in the seventeenth century as continental Europe began to recognize the economic potential of the Caribbean islands' agricultural productivity and natural resources: cotton, salt, indigo, tobacco, spices, exotic hardwoods, and sugar. It was not long thereafter that Spain's domination of the West Indies ceased. In 1600, the Dutch settled Saint Eustatius (Statia), and in 1621 they established the Dutch West India Company. In 1623, the English settled Barbados and Saint Christopher (Saint Kitts), and two years later, Nevis. By the mid-seventeenth century, the French had settled Martinique and Guadeloupe (the "Caribee Islands") and in 1664 King Louis XIV chartered the French West India Company. The Danish West India and Guinea Company, chartered by King Christian V of Denmark in 1670, took possession of Saint Thomas in 1672 and Saint John in 1717. Sixteen years later, Danish king Christian V purchased the island of Saint Croix from the French.

Possession of the West Indies was of tremendous military, economic, and political significance for the five European nations. All five colonizing countries were determined to monopolize the islands' productivity, and each looked with envy on the trade activity and territorial possessions of the others. During the colonial period, fierce and frequent battles were waged. Dominion changed so often that the Virgin Islands eventually became known as the "Land of Seven Flags"—a name that reflected the alternation of the nations ruling over them. Some of the islands changed hands so often that, at times, new governmental staff disembarked after an arduous journey from Europe to discover that their residences and their jobs had been captured by another country. Saint Lucia, for example, changed hands fourteen times between France and England before the English took final possession in 1814. Saint Martin/Saint Maarten changed hands sixteen times by 1817 and today is shared by both the French and the Dutch.

As it turned out, the West Indian islands did not possess the mineral riches of gold and silver that their conquerors had anticipated. Nevertheless, the European settlers soon discovered the islands' exceptional arability, and began to grow cotton, tobacco, and indigo. These early Caribbean "plantations" were comparable to small farms of today. In the fledgling year of 1691, Saint Thomas alone had 101 of these plantations, only five of which were devoted to sugarcane; at that early date, most grew cotton.

A turning point for the future of the islands came in 1640 when the Dutch "stole" the secret of sugarcane cultivation and processing from Brazil—where the Portuguese had kept it jealously guarded—and carried it to Barbados. Historically, it is believed that India was the first to process sugar. The Arabs then introduced it to the eastern Mediterranean around 600 A.D., and four hundred years later the Crusaders brought it back to Europe. Originally an aristocratic luxury, by the time Columbus discovered the Caribbean, sugar was on its way to becoming a common necessity, and the climate of the West Indies proved ideal for its cultivation. By the 1700's, all the West Indian islands began to prosper from the export of this "white gold" and its by-products, rum and molasses.

fig. 4. View from a Great House near Sainte-Marie on Martinique

Because of their wealth in the flow of international trade, lifeblood of the eighteenth century, and from the new crop of sugar sweetening the tongue of Europe and from the slave trade bringing labor to do the hot and heavy work on the sugar plantations, the islands were prizes for any nation greedy for the hard currency believed at the time to be the stuff of power.[3]

Sugar became the greatest treasure of the eighteenth century, and the trading and shipping of this valuable commodity to the mother country involved more than a simple ocean passage to Europe. The successful operation of these sugar plantations—the planting and harvesting of cane, and the manufacture and transport of the sugar—was of utmost concern to the planters. The plantation system was developed and a search for vast reserves of cheap labor ensued. Neither the European settlers nor the few remaining indigenous Indians were able to withstand the requisite labor-intensive fieldwork and the hot and humid tropical climate. The Africans, on the other hand, were acclimated to the tropical heat and humidity, and as a result, it was the African that was sought as an alternative. Slavery became the indispensable driving force behind the success of the plantation economy in the mid-eighteenth

6

century. As more plantations turned to sugarcane production, tens of thousands of enslaved Africans were shipped from regions in coastal and central West Africa. European countries built forts along the "Guinea" or "Gold" Coast to accommodate the slave trade. In total, over fifteen million Africans were brought to the New World during nearly three hundred years of slavery.

Several factors determined which of the two North Atlantic trade routes were used: the winds, the currents, the season, and market supply and demand. Ships that traveled by the first route often left Europe in the fall after the harvest loaded with manufactured goods and provisions: "meat (ox tongue), butter, beer, salt, bread, coarsely cracked grain such as wheat or barley, herbs, vinegar, brandy, rope, slave clothes, nails and sailcloth."[4] This route led southwest from Europe, followed the North Equatorial Current between the Azores and the Canary Islands, and reached the West Indies after approximately three months at sea. Having landed in the Caribbean, the ships were then loaded with sugar, molasses, mascavado (raw sugar), rum, cotton, and exotic timber (mahogany, lignum vitae, fustic). From the West Indies, the ships would either travel to North America or return to Europe. If a ship followed the Antilles Currents to the North Atlantic Gulf Stream, the journey to Europe was approximately four thousand miles and took approximately six to eight weeks. The trip to North America (more often made by the Dutch, English, and French rather than the Danish ships) was a three-week voyage to a port of call for the purpose of selling the slaves, timber, and sugar they had taken on in the Caribbean.

The first leg of the second route, known as the triangular trade route, originated in Europe, traveled along the Canary Current to the west coast of Africa and the Guinea coast. Having delivered a cargo of provisions to the slave ports of West Africa, the ships were then loaded with enslaved Africans and began their voyage to the West Indies. The term "middle passage" refers to the voyage of slave-laden ships—ten to twelve weeks across the Atlantic—from Africa to the West Indies. The third leg of the journey completed the triangle, either with a stop in North America or a direct return voyage to Europe.

During the colonial era, between the early 1700s and the 1850s when "sugar was king," thousands of sugar plantations were developed on the Caribbean islands, as large fortunes were amassed in tobacco, cotton, tropical woods, and especially sugar. Wealthy Europeans owned most of the island plantations, either as absentee owners or as relative newcomers to the islands. Often they viewed life on the islands as a necessary and temporary "exile," during which time they could effectively make a fortune and eventually return home to Europe. And make their fortunes they did. While riding with his prime minister, William Pitt, in Weymouth, England, King George III met up with a planter in an ostentatiously elaborate equipage. When the king discovered that it belonged to a Jamaican, he reportedly exclaimed, "Sugar, sugar hey? All that [from] sugar!"[5]

Not all the Europeans who immigrated to the islands were wealthy. Most were not accustomed to the finer things in life and had eagerly sailed to the West Indies to make their fortunes. In fact, most of the islands' plantocracy epitomized the definition of "nouveau riche" long before the phrase became part of the general parlance. The Scotch/Irish MacEvoy family was the paradigm of the plantation family dynasty. Having arrived on the island of St. Croix in 1751, Christopher MacEvoy had become one of the "most distinguished planters" on the island by the time he applied for Danish citizenship twenty-five years later. By 1804, his sons Michael and Christopher, Jr. owned over 1,000 slaves and 3,000 acres of fertile plantation land. The MacEvoys were synonymous with West Indian wealth and extravagance in turn-of-the-century Denmark. Christopher, Jr., who spent much of his time in Denmark while Michael managed the island estates, had a palace in Copenhagen and maintained a large country manor. He was appointed Chamberlain to the Royal Household and then fell from favor when he overstepped the royal prerogative of sporting an elaborate equipage with livery of six white chargers. Exiled for this faux pas, he returned to town several years later on a carriage pulled by six white mules. His humor earned him reentry into

fig. 7. An eighteenth-century Caribbean Great House on the island of Martinique

Introduced by the Dutch, the *sugar* windmills and animal

fig. 8. A sugarcane windmill at the Whim Museum, Frederiksted, Saint Croix. On the left is an animal mill, an earlier device for crushing sugarcane. Horses or oxen powered the animal mill. Tethered to an overhead boom, the animals walked a circular path, causing the boom to turn rollers to crush the cane.

fig. 9. Once the heart of the plantation, a stone sugar mill still stands, although the roundhouse and blades that would have surmounted it are gone. Sugarcane was brought in through the large archway. Inside, three

lignum vitae or iron rollers crushed the sugarcane to produce the juice, and then the crushed cane was disposed of through another archway. Thousands of these old sugar mills still stand on islands in the Caribbean.

fig. 10. A 25-foot waterwheel once powered the sugar mills on an estate on Saint Lucia.

10

mills were *once the heart* of *the sugar plantation.*

royal favor. This infamy aside, Christopher MacEvoy, Jr. was famous throughout Denmark for his ostentation—funded by the MacEvoy West Indian plantations. Today, one of these plantations, named Estate Whim after the eighteenth-century word for sugar mill, is a Saint Croix plantation museum.

Like the MacEvoys, other European settlers arrived on the West Indian islands in the late seventeenth through the early nineteenth centuries and created a society based on wealth and power. The income generated by sugar and its byproducts led to the construction of grand and opulent residences, called "Great Houses," which became public monuments to the planters' achievement. This grand style of living extended beyond the plantocracy; even those who held only a government post, a small plot of land, or a few slaves, were intent on living in an opulent style that reflected their newly gained social status. As such, architects were recruited to design the plantation great houses and palatial townhouses, and no expense was spared on these impressive homes.

On the English and Danish islands, homes were built from coral stone, which was taken from the surrounding reefs and favored for its softness and pliability. According to an account published in Copenhagen in 1758:

> ...the reefs surrounding the island produce a limitless supply of coral stone...the stones are brought from the sea to the land in the following manner: Two slaves row a boat from shore to the reef, or as it is called, canoe, where five to six other slaves are standing, breaking off the stones with thick wooden sticks. When the boat arrives they fill it with the stones. While the boat is returning to shore with those stones, the slaves loosen the other ones until the boat returns...[6]

Some homes were built partially of bricks brought as ships' ballast from overseas.

Typically, the interior and exterior walls were finished with a lime and sand plaster, which was fired from crushed coral stone and seashells, and mixed with water. In times of drought, molasses was sometimes used instead of water; and to this day, the walls may seep molasses.

The sugarcane plantations' great houses, island government offices, and merchant townhouses displayed the greatest concentration of wealth and of European influence, for these homes and offices were the planters', the merchants', and the government officials' testimonial to their success and their formal showcases of wealth, sophistication, and taste. The ex-European plantocracy of the West Indies wanted to recall a lifestyle comparable to the major European cities; Saint-Pierre, Martinique was referred to as the "Paris of the Antilles," and Bridgetown in Barbados strove to recreate London. It was this upper stratum of the sugar islands' plantation society that generated the demand for beautiful furnishings, which ultimately catalyzed the production of the unique furniture of the West Indies.

fig. 11. An interior of an island Great House; the English mahogany table was made by Benjamin Palmer Titter (w. 1799–1830) of London and Norwich, 1810–1820. It bears a brass plaque on each end that reads, "The New Constructed Occasional Table / by B. P. Titter / Inventor and Manufacturer." The table is surrounded by nineteenth-century English mahogany chairs. The American mahogany sideboard of c. 1840 and the English girandole mirror of c. 1820 above it were acquired with the house. The small mahogany cup (or cupping) table between the windows and the mahogany side chairs with vase-shaped splats are early nineteenth-century colonial West Indian. The English chandelier dates from c. 1820.

Furniture from the Islands

West Indian furniture is so unique in its design as to defy easy stylistic classification. In fact, it is often difficult to determine the age of island pieces because, as local craftsmen responded to changing styles abroad, in many cases they reinterpreted the forms and retained only some aspects of the originals. Designs were further altered by the addition of African motifs developed in relative isolation from the changing fashions of mainland and European furniture. Adding to the complexity was the occasional inter-island exchange of forms that was a direct result of itinerant cabinetmakers or of inter-island shipping.

It was imported furniture that first adorned the island great houses and urban mansions. Whether from England, Ireland, Denmark, Holland, Spain, France, or North America, these pieces were always of the latest style. The sophisticated nineteenth century ladies' work table shown here as fig. 13—designed to provide a compact, moveable storage space for sewing and writing paraphernalia—is an excellent example of the type of imported European furniture that the local craftsmen looked to when seeking inspiration for their West Indian versions. This table is Danish, from the early 1800s and has the rare distinction of retaining its

fig. 12. An example of the Spanish Baroque furniture crafted in the Caribbean, now in the Casa del Conde de Bayona in Havana, Cuba, which today houses the Museum of Colonial Art

13

14

fig. 13. A Danish work table made in the early nineteenth century of mahogany and pine. According to oral tradition, it was imported to Saint Croix.

fig. 14. Labels affixed to the pine bottom of the work table

opposite:
fig. 15. An eighteenth-century "dressing table of the sacristia (sacristy)" found in Cuba, an example of the weightiness characteristic of colonial Spanish furniture

original shipping labels. Affixed to the pine bottom board of the worktable, the labels indicate that the table was shipped from Copenhagen to the West Indies aboard the *Xenia* of the Albrechtsen line. The label reads as follows:

XENIA [name of ship]
VESTINDIEN [West Indies—Destination]
ALBRECHTSEN [Name of the shipping line]
DET FORENDE ["The Leading"—Refers to shipping Line]
DAMPSKIBSSELSKAB ["via"]
KOBENHAVN H [Copenhagen H]

Details such as the overhanging top and the flattened ball turning on this piece were absorbed into the vocabulary of the Caribbean craftsmen.

During the sixteenth and early seventeenth centuries, it was Spanish Baroque furniture that arrived initially, as Spain was the first to colonize the New World. This furniture was

carved with elaborate curvilinear motifs and had an overall weightiness similar to the Spanish colonial furniture found in Mexico and South America.

Later, during the eighteenth and nineteenth centuries, other European colonizing nations assumed the role of influencing the design of island furniture, as each brought its own culture's popular styles. Often, this succession created an evolving amalgamation of European styles; in furniture, as in art, there were no abrupt changes; one style overlapped another as a new style gradually replaced an earlier one.

The French were the arbiters of taste and design in the European community during this time. The Huguenots, who were the master craftsmen of the decorative arts in France, carried the French Baroque style to the Protestant states of Germany, England, and Holland when they fled France after Louis XIV's revocation of the Edict of Nantes in 1685 (which led to the persecution of Protestants). It was the French styles of the eighteenth and nineteenth centuries that influenced all other European fashion. In terms of Caribbean furniture, the island interpretations were generally simplified modifications—on a larger scale and with locally influenced ornamentation—of the homeland's styles, and constructed of the local exotic woods.

The Dutch version of Baroque-style furniture tended to be heavy, flamboyant, imposing, and monumental in appearance—seemingly designed for display rather than for comfort or function. In England, the Baroque movement developed into the Queen Anne style, a manner more restrained and simply curvilinear than its Dutch counterpart, and remarkable for the elegant graceful lines exemplified by the cabriole leg. Later, the Queen Anne style evolved into the asymmetrical, elaborate Rococo. By the mid-eighteenth century, the embellishments of the Rococo style became less favored and eventually fell out of vogue throughout Europe. Prompted by the archaeological discoveries at Herculaneum and Pompeii beginning in 1738, European designers began to introduce a Neo-Classical manner. Later, embellishment of this Neo-Classical style led to the Regency and Empire styles, after which various industrial revival fashions continued until the twentieth century.

As the product of a British colony, North American furniture was strongly influenced by English fashion, although simpler in design than that of the mother country. Most of the

fig. 16. A colonial French West Indian mahogany console from Balenbouche Estate, Saint Lucia

North American furniture that was exported to the West Indies came from the coastal cities of Philadelphia, Boston, New York, and Charleston. The New England colonies had also traded with the Caribbean islands, and since the middle of the seventeenth century had shipped them provisions and received timber and sugar from them.

Commerce between the North American ports in New England, New York, New Jersey, Pennsylvania, and the West Indies continued throughout the eighteenth century and well into the nineteenth, until the decline in the sugar industry. Furniture was shipped to the West Indies, both by order and as "venture" cargo. In 1791, according to American State Papers, "…56 carriages of coaches, chariots, phaetons and chairs were sent to the West Indies. These "carriages" contained sixty-two desks, fifteen bureaus, twenty-six sofas and settees, thirty-four tables, and six bedsteads. In the same year, four thousand Windsor chairs were shipped to the French West Indies…"[7] Outward-bound shipping manifests from the U. S. Bureau of Customs District of Philadelphia recorded that 52,311 individual pieces of furniture were exported from Philadelphia alone to the West Indies between 1820 and 1840.

Early references to North American furniture trading are very limited, and those that do exist seldom give more than a one-word description and an assigned value. English author Edward Joy, however, offers one of the most descriptive pieces of data:

> *The figures refer to qualities and not values and the destinations (on which the records give no information) include foreign islands. Additional exports were (in 1769 only) 75 cabinets (all from American colonies), and 12, 9, and 10 cases of drawers in 1770, 1771, and 1772 respectively (again all from the American colonies, except two in 1772). All these goods came from American ports along the whole length of the coast, from Piscataqua in the North to Savannah in the South. An analysis of the ports and their exports gives some interesting facts. Most of the desks and tables came from New Hampshire, Massachusetts and Rhode Island; 374 and 114 in 1771; and 536 and 157 in 1772. On the other hand, most of the chairs came from New Hampshire and Pennsylvania (mainly Philadelphia).*[8]

Armoires became *popular*

on the island because their airy

interiors were *less attractive* to tropical

mold, mildew, and *insects.*

fig. 19. An English West Indian mahogany sideboard in the Georgian manner, but with a distinctly large serpentine splashboard

fig. 20. An English-inspired colonial West Indian sofa table made of mahogany, part of the collection at Good Hope Plantation, Jamaica. The oil painting by Joseph Bartholomew Kidd (1818–89) hanging above the table shows the plantation in the nineteenth century. The floors are made of wild orange wood.

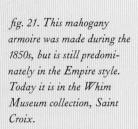

fig. 21. This mahogany armoire was made during the 1850s, but is still predominately in the Empire style. Today it is in the Whim Museum collection, Saint Croix.

opposite:
fig. 22. This chair found on Saint Vincent is an example of Empire-inspired colonial West Indian furniture.

21

It usually took a number of years before the newest fashion in furniture design from Europe or North America arrived in the West Indies, and in the general absence of design books, the bulk of the furniture that influenced island design as inspiration and model was that which was imported, particularly during the first half of the nineteenth century, the period of greatest wealth. Although there were early examples of Baroque- and Rococo-influenced furniture made in the islands, it wasn't until the third quarter of the eighteenth century—when the West Indies began its era of greatest prosperity—that the Neo-Classical and eventually the Empire styles became popular. The West Indian craftsman integrated many of the design motifs from these and subsequent imported styles, but as time passed, he never completely relinquished the Empire style, which was the last handcrafted imported style.

During the second quarter of the nineteenth century, Europe and North America had begun to rely on the less expensive machine production of furniture, which marked the end of the great era of handcraftsmanship. The inferior construction of mechanically mass-produced furniture was often hidden behind surface or applied carved decoration, but its low

price and easy availability were suitable for the market demand from the Industrial Revolution's growing middle class. The revival styles that immediately followed the Empire Period were the first to be generally machine-produced. Classical Revival pieces were characterized by straight columns, flat surfaces devoid of carving and often veneered, and scrolled legs and feet. The simple solid forms of this style, with their glistening French polished veneered surfaces, represented an attempt to recreate the lavishness of fine furniture in a mass-produced market.

In the West Indies, where there were few machines, little metalworking, and no steam power until later in the century, furniture continued to be completely handcrafted throughout the century. West Indian craftsmen were slow to adopt the nineteenth-century revival styles because early machine-made furniture relied heavily on mechanically cut thin veneers, curvilinear forms, and intricate carving that were easy to execute on a machine saw with a template, but were very time-consuming to execute by hand. When West Indians did copy these styles, they adopted only certain elements rather than creating faithful replicas of the original pieces. The fact that theirs was a handwork tradition contributed to the permanence of the copied Empire style in the West Indies, which had been the most popular in the days of prosperity on the islands, and was also evocative of that time.

The Rococo Revival and Renaissance Revival style furniture of the middle of the nineteenth century did influence West Indian craftsmen noticeably in the type of ornamentation and motifs they used, but these motifs were regionally adapted. An applied curvilinear form became a zoomorphic motif on many West Indian pieces, and carved vegetative motifs reflected the plant life of the islands, such as the hibiscus flower or banana leaves, instead of reproducing the ubiquitous European acanthus. The succeeding Renaissance Revival style, which reintroduced French Classical Revival forms from the sixteenth through the eighteenth centuries, led island craftsmen to go back to earlier geometric styles and to banish curvilinear forms. This straight-lined architectural furniture with its classical or Renaissance-inspired symmetrical design brought West Indian furniture full circle. From the eighteenth century's early Neo-Classical period to the last quarter of the nineteenth century, furniture

fig. 24. A mahogany carving of tropical foliate on a four-post bedstead headboard

fig. 25. A mahogany head-board of a four-post bed showing zoomorphic forms, Virgin Islands, c.1850

design made a circular progression away from and then back to representing classical architectural features such as door pediments, wall panels, straight shelves, and heavy cornices. The dominant Empire style never left West Indian design; it is perhaps more accurate to say that it was embellished and may have become heavier, but it never gave way completely to other styles.

Because island craftsmen reinterpreted and adapted the imported forms, examination and identification of colonial West Indian furniture is required to elucidate its precise contribution to the cabinetmaking craft. Analysis and correlation of its unique construction techniques distinguish Caribbean colonial furniture from its European and North American relatives. Upon examination of the craftsmanship of these pieces, the furniture student or connoisseur must look for distinguishing "signatures" and then compare these signatures to known construction techniques of dovetailing, joining, and turning.

One invariable sign of island regional craftsmanship is the unique practice of using mahogany as both primary and secondary woods or of placing mahogany veneer over solid mahogany secondary wood. Before the Industrial Revolution and the introduction of machinery, hand-sawn veneer measured as thick as one-sixteenth and one-eighth of an inch. Veneering mahogany was usually cut from the tree crotch as this produced the highest degree of contrast in light and dark wood grain, which is known as "figuration." Although veneering was used as decoration as far back as the seventeenth century, West Indian cabinetmakers did not begin to use it as such until the late 1700s.

26 27 28

Although other indigenous tropical hardwoods were used, mahogany was the furniture maker's wood of choice. In fact, during the eighteenth century, it was not only the most valuable timber tree in the West Indies, but also the world's premier cabinet wood. Reportedly, mahogany was introduced to England in 1595, when Sir Walter Raleigh presented Queen Elizabeth with a mahogany table. Legend has it that the first European furniture made of West Indian mahogany was crafted in the late 1600s in Spain in the Baroque style, and that the wood was taken from a dismembered Spanish galleon that had been constructed in the Greater Antilles. The botanical name for West Indian mahogany is *Swietenia mahogani*, a designation that distinguishes it from Honduran and American mainland mahogany.

A medium-sized to large deciduous tree with maximum size 40–60 feet in height and 3–4½ feet in trunk diameter. The trunk is usually short and has swollen or buttressed base when large, and produces a spreading, much-branched crown. . . . The heartwood is reddish, pinkish, or yellowish when freshly cut, gradually turning dark rich reddish brown. The wood is moderately hard, heavy and strong. It is very resistant to decay and to attack by dry-wood termites.

The wood is used chiefly for furniture, cabinet making, interior finish, and veneers, being easily worked and taking a beautiful polish. . . . Roots and stumps of large trees are especially prized for their irregular wavy grain. Considered superior in quality and durability to the wood of Honduras mahogany.[9]

fig. 26. Close inspection of this colonial West Indian armoire (after removing the veneer from the block at the upper left) shows the mahogany secondary wood, the thickness of the mahogany veneer used as primary wood, and a detail of dovetail construction.

fig. 27. Detail of a colonial West Indian mahogany bedstead showing indigenous satinwood and mahogany veneering

fig. 28. An example of the work of the Jamaican cabinetmaker, Ralph Turnbull, c. 1830

Roots and stumps of large trees are *especially prized.*

Upon arrival to the islands, the plantation owner had to clear his land first before sugar cane planting could begin:

. . . but a good business for the owner in that he could ship the precious lumber of lignum vitae and mahogany to Europe and at the same time have the fertile soil prepared for the planting of cotton, sugar or tobacco. In Europe there was a great demand for West Indian wood, and it is said that many a planter received more for his lumber than he had paid for the plantation.[10]

From the beginning of the eighteenth and throughout the nineteenth centuries the West Indian woodworker used other island tropical hardwoods to create articles that today are made of metal. The large gears, cogs, and rollers used in the first sugar mills were made of lignum vitae and thibet. Introduced by the Dutch, the sugar windmills and animal mills were constructed of limestone and were once the heart of the sugar plantation. The animal mill (an example of which can be seen at the left of fig. 8) was the oldest crushing system known in the West Indies. It first appeared in Guadeloupe in 1642, where it had been brought over by the Huguenots from Holland. The tropical hardwoods used in the mills were so dense and resistant to climate and insects that many of the handmade cogs, rollers, and gears can be found today relatively intact, in and around the plantation fields and sugar mill ruins. Carpenter tools, eating utensils, bowls, and dishes were also crafted of wood.

The growth of the sugar trade stimulated the building of island townhouses, churches, warehouses, and plantations, and thereby provided a demand for even more skilled house wrights and finish carpenters. In his book on the historic buildings of Saint Thomas, Frederick Gjessings mentions the craftsmanship reminiscent of fine cabinetmaking, seen in the interior of the Saint Thomas synagogue in Charlotte Amalie. "The mahogany pews and other joinery recall the fine furniture once made in the Danish West Indies."[11]

While it is possible in almost every case to positively identify a Caribbean island piece, even those that have been modified or repaired, it is far more difficult to identify the makers of the furniture of the West Indies. Few records exist from cabinetmaking shops, particularly in the eighteenth and nineteenth century when most of the craftsmen were enslaved, anony-

opposite:
fig. 29. A nineteenth-century colonial West Indian mahogany four-poster bed from the Lawaetz Museum at Little La Grange, a former nineteenth-century Great House

mous, and illiterate. With rare exception, there is no tradition of signing, labeling, or dating pieces in the islands until the twentieth century. Much of what we know has been passed down orally or comes from personal diaries or chronicles of the time.

The heritage of the West Indian cabinetmaker in most cases is African, although there are a few examples of European furniture makers traveling to the West Indies to work, such as Ralph Turnbull, who made furniture in Jamaica in the 1830s. For the Africans, formal education and training were either discouraged or forbidden (with the exception of the Danish islands), but the need for craftsmen to build and maintain the plantation great houses, estates, and infrastructures necessitated a steady, skilled labor supply. Every well-run plantation needed carpenters, and the woodworking trade provided an excellent opportunity not only for rough carpentry but also for woodturning, joining, carving, and cabinetmaking. By the mid-eighteenth century, there is evidence of a large number of slaves skilled in the trades.

31

32 and 33

fig. 30. The colonial West Indian mahogany tall-post bed of c. 1850 has boldly proportioned post and spindle turnings characteristic of beds made in the Virgin Islands. Beside it is a small West Indian mahogany press of c. 1840. These small presses were preferred over chests of drawers for the storage of clothes because they were airier and thus less conducive to mildew and mold. The West Indian mahogany mirror also dates from the nineteenth century.

fig. 31. A West Indian bedstead showing bold proportions of turning in the bedposts

fig. 32 (upper right). A mahogany tall-post bed made by Charles McFarlane, Saint Croix, 1860, with alternating convex and concave rope turning

fig. 33 (lower right). A West Indian bed made from courbaril with a frame tester and mosquito netting

We may justly assume that the *rocking* chair before 1800 was *rare*.

From the earliest times, it has been common here for masters to have the most able of their slaves trained in those mechanical arts whose practice was both necessary and useful to the development of their industry over the long run. Many years of experience have demonstrated that the Negroes do not lack the aptitude for these skills and that they often bring them to that degree of perfection, which has been established by white professionals. Thus, masons, carpenters, cabinet-makers, coopers, blacksmiths, tailors, shoemakers, and barbers are to be found among them.[12]

Once the island styles were developed, it was the local furniture, more than any foreign work that became a primary influence on other cabinetmakers of the region, as well as an incentive to perfect their skills. Island craftsmen tended to look to their own friends and competitors for stylistic ideas and influences, rather than to imported models. Among local

artisans there was occasionally a gentle rivalry in developing new refinements. For example, Charles McFarlane, a nineteenth-century woodworker with a shop in Frederiksted, Saint Croix, was best known for the artistically turned posts he created. After an exceptional turning or carving was executed, McFarlane placed the piece outside for the public's admiration. His contemporaries, Septimus McBean and Maxwell Plaskett, upon seeing the work, would rush back to their shops to attempt something superior.

Unquestionably, more four-post bedsteads have survived in the West Indies than any other form of colonial furniture. Early inventories often identify the type of wood used (mahogany) in beds, but a more complete description is rarely given. West Indian mahogany bedsteads are remarkable for their large size. A seemingly inexhaustible supply of timber allowed for massive, tall posts that were intricately turned and carved. Higher than other beds in that era, the rails on West Indian beds were usually over twenty-five to twenty-six inches from the ground, which intentionally placed the mattress at the level of the open windows and thereby exposed it to cool, tropical breezes.

When it comes to West Indian four-post bedsteads, there are as many different designs as there were colonizing countries and just as many variations on those designs. But generally, the beds had a number of things in common. The mattress, which was typically cotton sacking stuffed with coconut husk, was supported by mahogany slats that were five to six inches wide. Slats were cut and laid between the side rails at intervals of four to five inches to allow for substantial airflow. The slats were used instead of the

opposite:
fig. 37. Two examples of nineteenth-century Jamaican campeche *chairs*

below:
fig. 38. A Spanish colonial West Indian version of a nineteenth-century campeche *chair*

These chairs were designed with excessively *long arms*

so that the weary planter could elevate his legs on its arms,

which allowed the swelling in his feet and lower legs

to subside so that his *boots* could be removed.

opposite:
fig. 39. A room in the Whim Plantation Museum, Saint Croix. Most rocking chairs in the Danish West Indies have the curvilinear shape of these, an influence of North American imports.

fig. 40. A nineteenth-century thibet wood colonial West Indian planter's chair with fixed extended arms and upholstered cloth seat

fig. 41. A planter's chair with folding extending arms and hand-caned seat from the island of Trinidad

customary hemp rope and rope pegs used elsewhere because of the short life of hemp in the tropical climate. Beds that did not have elaborate canopies had frame testers. Each corner of the rectangular mahogany tester frame had a hole drilled through it so that it fit snugly on nails protruding from the tops of the four posts. While four-post beds with testers were popular in Europe and in North America for hanging fabric or drapery for privacy and warmth, in the tropics they were essential structures for holding mosquito netting. The netting protected the occupant from mosquitoes that carried malaria and yellow fever—the two most dreaded diseases during colonial times. "The most costly piece of furniture was generally the master's four-posted bed, its mattress stuffed with feathers, flock, or plantain leaves, a canopy overhead, and the sides hung with curtains to keep out the bad night air."[13]

Because of the heat and humidity, upholstered seating furniture was never popular on the islands. The mahogany récamiers, settees, and chairs were usually hand-caned to adapt to the weather; the open caning was airy and therefore decidedly more functional and overwhelmingly preferred. In Europe, caning became fashionable during the Empire period when Napoleon's military made use of campaign furniture that included caned seating pieces; caning thereby gained an exotic appeal that went beyond its decorative effect. When the West Indies were colonized, they were found to be rich in rattans, and, as both fashion and practicality dictated their use, caning became ubiquitous in the Caribbean basin. The caner's craft, along with that of the turner, became among the most important in the region.

About the mid-1830s caned furniture, so practical and comfortable in the tropics, came increasingly into use. The Neo-Rococo forms that in northern regions were generously cushioned and upholstered with horsehair and velvet were fitted with caning in round or oval carved mahogany frames and usually protected by antimacassars. Less expensive seats, though also of mahogany, had backs and seats of rush.[14]

The caned rocking chair, found throughout the Caribbean, was undoubtedly a popular form. Historically used in every room of the house and in the offices of merchants and government officials, the chair was designed for comfortable, cool seating; one simply had to rock the chair to produce a cooling airflow. Whereas in North America and Europe it was highly unusual to have rocking chairs grouped around tables in parlors, it was quite common to have such formations in the West Indies. The center of the room was a popular place to gather as it was the spot that received the cross-flow of cool tropical breezes from multiple windows. Woven caning used in chair seats and backs facilitated the free flow of air, thus combating the sultry tropical heat.

The rocking chair as we know it today probably originated in North America, a fact that was established early in the twentieth century by Irving Lyon in his discussion of the first recorded rocking chairs in the 1770s:

It may be fairly assumed that the two rocking chairs described there were of local conception and origin, not invented but rather adapted from the rocking cradle by the ingenious Yankee, perhaps for the use of children or invalids. It seems a good guess that the same ingenuity cropped out in different places from the same suggestion and led to the application of rockers to chairs in Philadelphia, Ipswich and other places.[15]

There is no mention of examples of eighteenth century rocking chairs in the West Indies, which would support Dr. Lyon's theory that the rocking chair was essentially a nineteenth-century form. "From all the evidence and lack of evidence, we may justly assume that the rocking chair before 1800 was rare, there for a special need."[16] It was during the first quarter of the nineteenth century that the "rocking chair did become established in general use"[17] in North America. While the basic form remained constant, the rocking chair styles varied from island to island.

Just as popular and as commonplace was the West Indian planter's chair, referred to throughout the Caribbean as a "lazy man's chair." While this type of chair is associated with the Caribbean sugar plantation, it is also related to tropical colonial chairs from around the world. Different versions are found in Sri Lanka, Indonesia, Mexico, and the Philippines. In Sri Lanka and India, which both the Portuguese and the English colonized, two styles of colonial planter's chairs are found. The Portuguese chair is very low, extremely reclined, and has long extended arms; the majority of these chairs were made of rosewood and had hand-

42

fig. 42. A mahogany parlor press, Saint Croix, early nineteenth century. The press is in the Whim Plantation Museum, a former Great House on an eighteenth-century sugar plantation on Saint Croix.

opposite:
fig. 43. A nineteenth-century French-inspired colonial West Indian armoire from Balenbouche Estate, Saint Lucia

woven caned seats. The second, English-influenced style had larger proportions, and was usually made of teak, with wide folding arms that extended to become leg rests. This latter type sits more upright than the former and has the same flat-reed woven caned seat.

The Dutch had their own version of the planter's chair in Indonesia, their colony in the East Indies, which were once known as the Spice Islands. The East Indian version type is more upright than the Caribbean one, is smaller in its proportions and has folding, extended arms. Still made today, East Indian chairs were made of teak and hand-caned. When the Spanish colonized the Philippines, they created yet another version of the planter's chair. Large like the Anglo-Indian, but sitting more upright than the folded-arm style from that region, Philippine chairs often featured hand-carved Baroque-style decoration on the crest rail. They were made from different indigenous woods, were hand-caned, and they differed

These tradesmen—blacksmiths, coopers, masons, carpenters, and cabinetmakers—

were free men who had acquired skills while enslaved on the estates.

in functionality from the other colonial versions in that they seldom had either fixed extended or folding arms on which the sitter's legs could be rested. Similar to this Philippine chair is the "campeachy" *(campeche)* chair or "Mexican siesta" chair (see fig. 64). The major difference between these last two examples is that the latter chair always has a leather upholstered seat rather than one that is hand-caned.

The West Indian form developed as a result of the influence of both Dutch and English colonists who brought the design from India and the Dutch East Indies. These chairs were designed with excessively long arms so that the weary planter could elevate his hot and swollen legs after a full day of surveying the sugarcane fields on horseback. In a posture that mirrored being astride a horse, the planter reclined in his chair, and rested his feet on its arms, which allowed the swelling in his feet and lower legs to subside so that his boots could be removed. Some planter's chairs were even crafted with a container for ice beneath the derriere to further cool and assuage the discomfort of extensive riding in the heat.

Another common form throughout the Antilles was the armoire, which, historically, was a domestic cupboard used first in France in the Gothic period. By the eighteenth century, as household inventories of the time make clear, every prosperous European home included an armoire. It was not until the turn of the nineteenth century that armoires (more often called wardrobes in the English and Dutch islands) became popular on the islands. Because their airy interiors were less attractive to tropical mold, mildew, and insects, armoires and parlor presses (small armoires) were used for clothes and linen storage more often than chests-of-drawers. West Indian craftsmen began to produce armoires first on the French islands; the Danish and English islands then followed.

The games table is another form often found in the islands. Called "gaming tables," "card tables" and "games tables," this term refers specifically to tables introduced in the eighteenth century that were designed for four people for playing board or card games such as whist. The European games table prototypes were often made with reversible tops, inlaid with

above:
fig. 45. A nineteenth-century cabinetmaking shop showing a workbench and lathe, from the Whim Plantation Museum collection, Saint Croix

opposite:
fig. 44. Cabinetmaker Harris Lionel from Mon Gouge, Saint Lucia

chess and backgammon boards on either side. Many West Indian games tables appear in inventory listings throughout the late eighteenth and nineteenth centuries, most frequently on the English islands. A Lutheran minister who visited the West Indies in 1740 described how colonial women spent their time: "White women are not expected to do anything here except drink tea and coffee, eat, make calls, play cards, and at times sew a little."[18] Often made in pairs, the island games tables were placed against a wall when not in use. As with other furniture forms, the first

fig. 46. A unique West Indian mahogany games table found on Jamaica

opposite:
fig. 47. A pair of gaming tables, Saint Croix, c. 1860, and a cedar chest on frame, Bermuda, eighteenth century. The gaming tables are mahogany and were originally in the Great House of Castle Nuggent Plantation on Saint Croix.

games tables were imported and used as templates for the later West Indian adaptations, which ranged from the restrained to the elaborately turned.

By the middle of the nineteenth century, the emancipation of the slaves and a dwindling demand for sugarcane began to bring the plantation era of opulence and prosperity to an end. The invention of processing sugar from beets meant the decline of sugarcane profits, and the abolition of slavery led to the decline in the labor force. As a result, the number of viable plantations decreased, as did the importation of high-style furniture to the islands. Increasing numbers of middle class families could not afford imported furniture and sought pieces made locally by island tradesmen instead. There are a only few general descriptions that help us to visualize a typical nineteenth-century middle class island home. Charles Edwin Taylor's mid-nineteenth-century observations in his *Leaflets from the Danish West Indies* include a lengthy description of one of these West Indian households:

> *The houses are not often built of more than two stories. Prudent builders make the upper story of wood, and the lower of brick or mason work. This is to guard against earthquakes and hurricanes, two reminders of the instability of earthly things that are not always welcome in the tropics. Each window is provided with strong shutters and hurricane bars. As a rule there are no knockers or bells attached to the door of entrance so you signify your presence by rapping with the hand or walk in, just according to the footing of intimacy upon which you stand with the family. It is difficult to give an idea of the interior...The furniture is substantially made of solid mahogany and is prettily*

Hand-carved motifs used as decoration on furniture retained an African influence.

fig. 48. A hand-carved stylized pineapple column on a
Dutch West Indian armoire.
Notice also the silver dove
escutcheon.

fig. 49. An example of the
definition in colonial West
Indian turning and the
decorative pineapple motif

opposite:
fig. 50. An English 1840s
mahogany games table from
Annandale Plantation,
Jamaica

draped with showy muslin curtains and mosquito nets…A magnificent mahogany press, and a chair or two, complete the furniture of the sleeping apartments. A fine mahogany press is the pride of every Creole beauty.[19]

These tradesmen—blacksmiths, coopers, masons, carpenters, and cabinetmakers—were free men who had acquired skills while enslaved on the estates. Free to establish their own businesses, they began to move into towns and villages, and by the third quarter of the nineteenth century, the freed West Indian had become a major labor force. Unfortunately, there are no surviving private records from these small local cabinet shops, but there does remain a sufficient amount of furniture that illustrates the close adherence to previously popular styles and imported prototypes.

During the last half of the nineteenth century, as factory assembly lines became the rule in furniture-making, craftsmen in Europe and North America began to lose their skill in making whole pieces. The ability to produce one furniture part or to perform one task in an assembly line became more important than broad-based craftsmanship. This did not occur in the West Indies.

Thus, one of the unique features of West Indian furniture is that it remained a craftsmanship tradition. Whereas Europe and North America had largely switched to machine production by the mid-nineteenth century, West Indians continued to make their furniture in the traditional manner; turning, for example, was still done on a manually powered lathe (see fig. 44). Carving skills were passed down from father to son and from master to apprentice, from the colonial era to the twentieth century. Similarly, the hand-carved motifs used as decoration on furniture retained the African influence in the depiction of tropical flora, fauna, and shells throughout this period. The continued importation of Africans during the eighteenth and most of the nineteenth centuries (despite the European decree banning the slave trade) reinforced the African carving traditions and kept these decorative images (serpents, flowers, nutmeg, melons, palm fronds, pineapples, sandbox fruit, and banana leaves) fresh and meaningful to generations of craftsmen.

By the turn of the twentieth century, furniture production had dropped considerably and by the middle of the century the few remaining cabinetmaker shops survived on repairs, recaning, and jobs that required limited amounts of carpentry and cabinetry skill.

The furniture made by the African West Indian craftsmen, joiners, turners, and cabinetmakers is one of the most meaningful aspects of the material culture that survives from the colonial period and, as such, it provides insight into the creative and practical lives of the people who made it. The furniture communicates to us in a way that the records cannot.

[O]ld furniture . . . speaks to me in a way that no other medium quite equals.
A piece of furniture says something about the man who made it and the man who used it that we do not find out about from the verbal documents to which most historians address themselves. In the way that a craftsman ran a groove or carved a flower or even planed a board . . . we can sense whether he respected what he was making or was merely working for wages. From the pro-portional relationships that the craftsman designed his pieces of furniture to express, we come into contact with this mind, his education and more—his vision.[20]

As the contemporary author John Vlach has said in reference to craftsmen's contributions, "In many instances we have seen that black creations in the United States were an extension of decorative, expressive, and pragmatic concepts initiated in the West Indies."[21] The volume and quality of furniture from the late eighteenth and nineteenth centuries is indicative of the degree of training the African craftsmen of the islands received in the cabinetmaking art.

Part 2

ISLAND STYLES

Spanish

During his first voyage to the New World, Columbus sailed to Cuba and stopped on the island's north-eastern coast where he recorded in his journal:

> *The banks of the rivers are embellished with lofty palm trees, whose shade gives a delicious freshness to the air, and the birds and the flowers are uncommon and beautiful. I was so delighted with the scene that I had almost come to the resolution of staying here for the remainder of my days; for believe me, Sire, these countries far surpass all the rest of the world in beauty and convenience.*[22]

Spain soon discovered that the West Indies were invaluable, not for the precious metals they had hoped to find, but for their strategic position as a gateway to the expanding western empire. Spain concentrated her West Indian settlements in the Greater Antilles: Cuba, Hispaniola, Puerto Rico, and Jamaica (which later fell under British rule in 1655).

The first structures the Spanish built on these islands were defensive fortifications, many of which continue to stand today as reminders of Spain's continual battle against other European invaders. Because Spain conquered with the cross as well as the sword, cathedrals, churches, convents, and chapels were among the earliest structures as well. For example, the

fig. 51. Gallery of the upper floor of the Palacio de los Capitanes Generales, built between 1776 and 1791. The palace is the site of the Museo de la Ciudad de la Habana.

The West Indies were a gateway to the expanding Spanish empire.

opposite:
fig. 52. In old San Juan, Puerto Rico, this palatial townhouse shows designs for "maximum cooling effect."

fig. 53. Intricate wrought-iron grille-work characteristic of the Spanish islands

cathedral of Santo Domingo on Hispaniola was built in 1540 and is the oldest recorded use of mahogany in construction (some of its ecclesiastical sculptures date as early as 1514).

Before the Spanish completed its forts, an "urban" plan was developed for the island towns of Santo Domingo in Hispaniola, San Juan in Puerto Rico, Spanishtown in Jamaica, and Havana in Cuba. In accordance with ecclesiastic and royal directives from the mother country, streets were arranged in grid formation. The centrally located main square, which was the hub of social life, consisted of military headquarters and barracks, a cathedral or church, and official government offices.

Santo Domingo was the first capital of the New World and the first to have a fort, cathedral, and university. Hispaniola's economy was based primarily on the exportation of gold, but then quickly became the ideal departure base for the conquistadors. It was from Santo Domingo that Ponce de Leon sailed toward Puerto Rico, that Hernando Cortez left to discover Mexico, and that Diego Velázques departed to colonize Cuba.

By the end of the sixteenth century, the Spanish realized that although the supply of gold was dwindling, the agricultural potential of the islands was extraordinary. At the same time, they were constructing some of the first Spanish colonial Baroque buildings. The earliest colonial houses, although not nearly as large as those built a century later, were of dignified proportions. The homes were enhanced with arches, shuttered doorways, intricately carved woodwork and balconies—all typical architectural elements of Spanish colonial homes of this period. Spanish colonial architecture is esthetically distinctive within the realm of the West Indies. As on other islands, architectural design took into consideration the tropical weather conditions: the intense heat of the sun and the torrential rain.

At the beginning of the colonial period many of the first homes were built on a palatial scale, with patios, upper galleries, double arcades, and balconies that were clearly influenced by the

opposite:
fig. 54. Palacio de los Capitanes Generales, now the Museo de la Ciudad de la Habana

above:
fig. 55. Spanish colonial Neo-Classical architecture, the Palacio de Justo Cantero, Trinidad, Cuba

opposite:
*fig. 56. Interior of the
Palacio de Justo Cantero,
Trinidad, Cuba, built
in the late 1820s*

Mudéjar style that was then popular in Southern Spain, especially in Seville. There are also numerous examples of Mudéjar-style churches, cathedrals, and municipal buildings from early Cuba, Puerto Rico, and the Dominican Republic. Mudéjar was a Moorish style adopted from Andalusia in the seventeenth and eighteenth centuries, a legacy of the Moors who occupied Spain from the eighth to the fifteenth centuries. The term is usually used to describe architecture, but it also refers to furniture in the Hispano-Moresque style with similar ornamentation.

Once the colony was established it began to import furniture from Spain, which was being reproduced by local craftsmen; these pieces exhibited the Mudejar influence that was fashionable at the time. They included "friar's armchairs" (*sillón frailero*), massive embossed leather chests, many-drawered *vargueno* desks, and a dais, the largest item in the family home, serving as a work area by day and a sleeping couch by night.[23]

The Hispano-Moresque is a decorative style that evolved from the art of the Moslems in Christian Spain or of Christians working within the Spanish Moslem tradition. (Strictly speaking, the term refers to the work of Moslems who remained in Spain after it was reclaimed from Islamic rule.)

The mansions in the Spanish colonies in the West Indies contained lofty and finely carved wooden coffered ceilings, tiled floors, and shuttered balconies, all designed for maximum cooling effect. The combination of Moorish and European features that dominated the towns' architecture embodied the essential Spanish style of the colonial period. This unique Spanish Baroque style can also be seen in the architectural details such as the shape of the windows, their grilles, the undulating moldings, and wooden balusters.

During the 1700s, with the growth of the sugar industry, the Spanish colonies became more than commercial way stations and military outposts as they began to prosper economically and socially. Unlike other European colonists, the Spaniards built their palatial mansions in towns, away from their *ingenios* (sugar plantations) and *cafetales* (coffee plantations). "It must be emphasized that the wealthy owners of the ingenios and cafetales did not make their home on the plantations that earned them their fortunes. The houses on the plantations were used simply as 'pied-à-terres' when they came to inspect the work on their estates."[24]

Through the nineteenth century, as wealth increased, the opulent homes of planters, merchants, government officers, and European aristocracy abounded. Havana's richest man, Miguel de Aldama, built Aldama Place as "a monument to King Sugar."[25]

As more luxurious furniture appeared during the final period of Spanish domination, forms and ornamentation varied but caned backs and seats remained. "…[A] particular favorite was the rocking chair, so congenial to tropical languor. But the typical San Juan home kept its traditional simplicity, decorated with imports from Spain, France, the United States, South America, and other Caribbean islands, as well as with occasional furniture made locally.…"[26]

Many of these palatial townhouses remain in cities throughout Cuba, but there remains little trace of the residences on either the *ingenios* or *cafetales*, which were destroyed either during the War of Independence in the late nineteenth century or during the reorganization of agricultural systems in the last half of the twentieth century under Fidel Castro.

The Baroque and Rococo architectural styles in Santo Domingo, Havana, and San Juan eventually became more refined, with finer and lighter classical lines and more subtle decoration. Later, these "sugar palaces" boasted tall pillars, internal patios, galleried arcades with columns, balconies with intricately carved arches, and shuttered doorways. Typical of the nineteenth century, the decorative details in Spanish colonial architecture ranged in style from the Baroque and Rococo to the Neo-Classical.

In Puerto Rico, colonial homes have many of the same architectural components: street-side balconies, verandas, shuttered louvered windows, jalousies, and brightly painted stucco walls. Additionally, the Puerto Rican homes commonly had open courtyards, often with a well or a fountain. The interiors were replete with mahogany beams and vaulted doorways.

Initially, the Spanish *sacarocracia* or sugar aristocrats, who were comparable to other "down island" (i.e. the Lesser Antilles) planters, also imported their furnishings, which were then copied.

The old families of Trinidad had become extremely rich during the first decades of the nineteenth century, and frequently had their furniture brought over from Europe or the United States. Many of these imported pieces were copied by local craftsmen and were to be seen in all of Cuba's most opulent homes.[27]

opposite:
fig. 57. Interior of a palatial townhouse in Old San Juan, Puerto Rico

above:
fig. 58. A Spanish chair with tooled leather seats and backrests with metal studs

overleaf:
fig. 59. A suite of muebles de medallión, *showing the medallion-shaped backs of settees and chairs*

fig. 60. A Spanish colonial room setting, showing a sitting room and dining room, Cuba

opposite:
fig. 61. Glazed tiles with
garlands of pink roses set off
a pair of medallión *chairs*

overleaf:
fig. 62. A group of Spanish
colonial Renaissance revival
pieces, including "geometric"
classical-shaped seating fur-
niture

fig. 63. A view of the private
dispatch room showing late
seventeenth- and early eigh-
teenth-century furniture in
the Palacio de los Capitanes
Generales Museo de la
Ciudad de la Habana

The sugar barons were not alone in acquiring wealth; the Spanish merchants also shared in it.

The merchants' houses all followed a pattern:

The entrances are very spacious, the staircases as regal as those in Stafford House in London [known today as Lancaster House], the floors are marble, the walls are covered in azulejos or small glazed tiles and the banisters are made of iron. The rooms are twenty feet high, with exposed beams, the doors and windows are huge, and the furniture is elaborate and solidly made. Here the merchant or banker sits, in white trousers and elegantly shod. He undoes his white jacket, loosens his tie and smokes cigars, surrounded by luxury and sheltered from the sun.[28]

The earliest recorded historical mention of furniture on the Spanish islands referred to sixteenth-century "Spanish chairs," which had tooled leather seats and backrests with metal (usually copper) studs to secure the leather. The chairs were exported from the Spanish islands and from South America to other West Indian islands and to North America. This rustic chair, the *taburete,* became a standard piece during the early seventeenth century. The paneled wardrobe was also common to all households on Cuba. Generally, the wardrobes stood on flattened ball feet and featured decorative geometric motifs that mimicked those found on doors, windows, and roofs.[29]

According to Adolfo de Hostos:

Up to the 1830's, the parlor would be equipped with heavy furniture of solid mahogany, all elaborately carved: marble-topped pedestal tables, chairs upholstered in horsehair of leather, and folding game tables. For the bedrooms enormous mahogany double beds with four turned posts were imported from Curaçao, or field beds were fitted with wooden frames above for curtains or mosquito nets; later metal beds were imported from Europe. Large mahogany wardrobes and chests of drawers matched the bedsteads. Other amenities acquired in the first third of the 1800's include glass hanging lanterns and table lanterns, brass and silver candlesticks and hurricane shades, shelf clocks, Sevres porcelain vases, silver tableware, large framed mirrors, books, and keyboard instruments.[30]

65

66

opposite:
fig. 64. An early nineteenth-century mahogany and leather campeche *chair*

fig. 65. Detail of Spanish colonial Empire period carving on a mahogany console

fig. 66. A French-influenced nineteenth-century Spanish West Indian mahogany and caned love-seat

The Cubans made good use of island *timbers:* ebony, mahogany, and rosewood.

opposite:
fig. 67. A Spanish colonial West Indian wardrobe

overleaf:
fig. 68. A nineteenth-century Rococo revival mahogany table with marble top

fig. 69. Doors such as these, called mamparas, *used to separate rooms and encourage privacy, are a decorative and architectural element found only on the Spanish islands.*

Throughout the nineteenth century, a great deal of mahogany and cane furniture was produced in suites on Cuba and Puerto Rico and it followed every revival fashion. The *meubles de medallión* was a term that referred to seating furniture that incorporated carved medallion-shaped backs, which was popular during the 1850s Rococo Revival. Twenty years later, when the Renaissance Revival fashion was most popular, the carved medallion shapes were replaced with geometric, classical-shaped backs and seats.

In short, these were mansions fit for elegant, gracious living, complemented by superb furniture.

Side by side with the numerous pieces of furniture and artifacts that were imported from abroad, it was usual to place other pieces made in Cuba. Cuban furniture is primarily differentiated by its use of the island's native timbers: cedar, ebony, mahogany, rosewood, and others. It includes tried and tested objects of local use, such as rocking chairs, comadritas *(armless rockers),* tinajeros *for water filtering and cooling, and smoking chairs. . . . [T]he rocker suited the Cuban temperament to perfection. It is constantly evoked by travelers who were bewitched by the image of Havana beauties rocking back and forth, lazily fanning themselves beside trays of cool drinks and tropical fruit. As for Empire-style furniture made in Cuba, like* escaparate *wardrobes, it is charmingly provincial and well worth appreciation. Meanwhile beds were increasingly replacing lined cots, couches were coming into vogue, and sewing cabinets appeared. All these items reflected the influence of neoclassicism, largely as a result of greater commerce and exchange with the United States.*[31]

Dutch

The first threat to Spanish dominion came from the Dutch. But unlike their adversaries, the Dutch preferred commerce to military and territorial conquest. The three southern Windward islands of Saint Maarten, Saint Eustatius, and Saba, together with the three southern Leeward islands of Curaçao, Bonaire and Aruba constitute the Netherlands Antilles. The Dutch arrived on the West Indian Islands in the first decade of the 1600s. Renowned for their aggressive mercantilism in the fifteenth and sixteenth centuries, they were the principal sea traders off the Atlantic Coast of Europe and West Africa. Initially the Dutch were drawn to the Caribbean for the vital commodity of salt, which was used for preserving fish. The export of fish was a major industry in Holland, and there were plentiful newly discovered salt ponds off the coast of Venezuela. The early Dutch salt ships also traded in tobacco, sugar, and slaves, and as mentioned earlier, the Dutch are credited with bringing the technology of sugar processing from Brazil to Barbados in the mid-seventeenth century. In 1634, the Dutch took the Spanish port of Santa Ana and renamed it Willemstad. Shortly after, they acquired the nearby islands of Aruba and Bonaire to provide protection for Curaçao. In the following years, the purveyance of slaves to Spanish, Portuguese, English, and French settlements made Curaçao one of the largest and busiest commercial centers and slave markets in the West Indies.

fig. 70. *The Penha building in Willemstad, with its elegant curvilinear and curlicued cartouchelike gable, is an example of the early eighteenth-century Dutch Rococo style.*

72

Willemstad's architecture
is unmistakably Dutch,
directly copied from
the architectural styles
that developed in the
seventeenth century in
Amsterdam and Rotterdam.

fig. 71. The nineteenth-
century Dutch colonial West
Indian Neo-Classical style
can be seen both in land-
huizen (land houses) and
in the merchants' luxurious
townhouses.

fig. 72. Schrijnwerkerstraat,
or Cabinetmaker Street,
Otrobanda, Willemstad,
Curaçao

opposite:
fig. 73. The mahogany
pulpit of the Fort church on
Curaçao, made in the Rococo
style, by Pieter de Mey, 1769

By the mid-seventeenth century the Dutch West India Company had taken full possession of their islands from the Spaniards who had neglected these colonies in favor of expeditions to Mexico and Peru, which yielded troves of the precious metals of gold and silver. The Dutch "A-B-C" islands are arid, flat and almost entirely unarable; as a result, commerce and shipping formed the backbone of the economy. The Dutch settlers established slave centers on these islands located on the Spanish shipping routes, such as Willemstad, the capital of Curaçao, and a port of contraband trading.

Willemstad's architecture is unmistakably Dutch, as characterized by detailed brickwork, curvilinear cartouchelike gables, decorative red-tile roofs, and ornate dormer pediments. The two- and three-story townhouses and warehouses were directly copied from the architectural styles that developed in the seventeenth century in Amsterdam and Rotterdam. With the exception of adding arcaded verandas to the townhouses and painting them bright colors, the Dutch in Willemstad did little to develop an indigenous architectural style that was more congruous with the tropical climate than to their mother country. Outside of town, on the colonial plantation residences, the *landhuizen* (land houses) architecture was formal and grand, more in the later Neo-Classical style, and made greater use of verandas and shuttered windows to promote airflow and combat the heat.

The unique commercial development of another Dutch island, Saint Eustatius, illustrates Holland's successful mercantilism and the tremendous importance of trade to the West Indies. "Statia" was centrally located within the Caribbean, and was therefore perfectly positioned for maximum commercial exposure. Declared a free port by the Netherlands, Statia became the crossroads for trade between Europe and North America and the other Caribbean islands. Unimpeded by duties or exclusivity regulations, Statia was also a center for contraband trading. In addition to its advantageous geography, Statia possessed a harbor that could shelter over two hundred ships. These attributes made Saint Eustatius the richest

73

75

fig. 74. The interior of a
Dutch colonial landhuis,
with an early nineteenth-
century mahogany console
and a cedar armoire in the
background

fig. 75. Dutch delft tobacco
jars, each representing the
island from which the tobacco
was collected

The larger, heavier ornamental

elements found on West Indian armoires

were inspired by Dutch Caribbean pieces.

76

77

fig. 76. A nineteenth-century mahogany corner cabinet, one of a pair made to house the medical instruments for Dr. Nicolas Rojer, whose face is believed to be carved along the pediment

fig. 77. An eighteenth-century Dutch West Indian mahogany Kas (large wardrobe) or cupboard. The bun feet, large cornice, and molded panel doors are typical of the island Dutch Baroque cupboards.

fig. 78. An early nineteenth-century Dutch West Indian mahogany pillared armoire with locally crafted silver escutcheons

port in the West Indies and it quickly became known as the "Golden Rock." In a speech in 1781, Edmund Burke stated:

> *It had no produce, no fortifications for its defense, nor martial spirit nor military regulations....Its utility was its defense. The universality of its use, the neutrality of its nature was its security and its safeguard. Its proprietors had, in the spirit of commerce, made it an emporium for all the world....Its wealth was prodigious, arising from its industry and the nature of its commerce.*[32]

Saint Eustatius gained further recognition as the first foreign government to recognize independent United States. On November 16, 1776, with the ink on the Declaration of Independence barely dry, the brigantine *Andrea Doria* of the new Continental Navy sailed into the harbor below Fort Orange and fired a salute, which the Dutch promptly returned. Five years later, still infuriated by the Dutch salute to the new U.S. flag, British Admiral George Rodney sacked Saint Eustatius' port in retaliation.

Salt ponds also attracted the Dutch to Saint Maarten, and in 1631 the "West Indische Company" settled there and added this island to its colonies. Spain recaptured St. Maarten and kept it until 1648 when the Dutch and French returned, and an agreement was signed on Mont des Accords. Over the next century, the island changed hands many times between the Dutch, French, and English. The second half of the eighteenth century brought sugar plantations and prosperity, which lasted until the third quarter of the nineteenth century.

Although furniture was made for the Dutch settlers in the Caribbean islands, pieces made there were few compared to those produced in Holland's other colonial possessions in India, South Africa, Sri Lanka, and Indonesia, where there were longer and more advanced histories of indigenous craftsmanship. Early Dutch colonial Caribbean furniture is highly distinctive in its design, materials, and construction. Because Curaçao

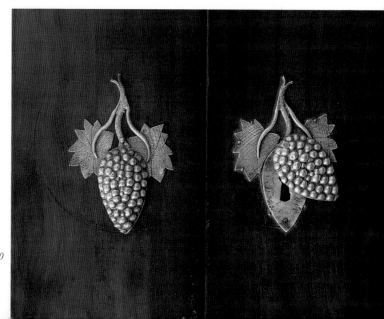

fig. 81. A unique colonial nineteenth-century mahogany settee. The lyre-shaped back and paw feet exemplify the Empire influence on the Dutch islands.

opposite:
fig. 82. A Dutch West Indian sideboard, colloquially referred to as a "water table," with serpentine splash-board and intricately turned legs

81

opposite:
fig. 83. A Dutch West Indian cedar washstand with serpentine splash-board and towel rails in curved supports

fig. 84. A late nineteenth-century Dutch West Indian mahogany dresser with applied molding, with a mirror and marble top influenced by the Renaissance Revival style

fig. 85. A Dutch colonial West Indian mahogany games table

opposite:
fig. 86. A mahogany "lyre"
hat stand with "boka di lora"
pegs. Another example can
be seen on p. 100.

was a large commercial port, it was exposed to furniture imported not only from Europe, but from South America and other Caribbean islands as well.

As in architecture, the Dutch craftsmen copied faithfully the Baroque style of seventeenth-century Holland. As on other Caribbean islands, there is little information about the individual Dutch furniture craftsmen and their trade before the nineteenth century. Presumably, they were less skilled and had cruder tools than their counterparts in the Netherlands. The craftsmen, therefore, steered away from more sophisticated European forms, and so curved stiles replaced the characteristic Dutch "bombe" form. On cabinets, doors were used rather than drawers, not because of their simpler construction, but also because they stood less of a chance of warping in the humid climate.

The first mention of a furniture maker in the Dutch West Indies appeared only when Pieter de Mey crafted the mahogany *hekhal* (Holy Ark) in the Mikve Israel Emanuel synagogue in Curaçao in 1709. Pieter de Mey's grandson of the same name was an accomplished cabinetmaker as well, and was reported to have constructed the mahogany pulpit of the Fort church in the Rococo style in 1769 (see p. 91).

Early inventories indicate that mahogany and cedar were the most widely used woods. The *kas*—a large wardrobe or cupboard—was a common Dutch form that consisted of two doors and pear-shaped or "bun" feet. The cupboards made on the Dutch islands were of mahogany and were not painted, unlike those made in Holland and in the Dutch North American colony of New Amsterdam (now New York), which were made of less exotic woods. Another form, the mahogany cabinet, was modeled after the Dutch Rococo cabinet that was typically decorated with stylized ornaments and had a contoured cornice with cresting and ledges for displaying jars or vases.

The Dutch style was clearly influential on islands near Saint Kitts, Nevis and Saint Thomas during the height of the plantation era. The larger, heavier ornamental elements found on Caribbean pieces, such as the large applied bulbous split turnings, are found on armoires in and around these islands. These heavier elements were inspired by Dutch Caribbean pieces, which was the most ponderous of the West Indian styles.

fig. 87. A Dutch West Indian water filter cabinet, or stila. *Rainwater from the lower basin was poured into the upper one. This basin made of porous stone cleans the water, which leaks slowly into the middle basin. The middle basin can also be used as a cooler when food is placed against it to prevent spoiling. The bottom jar contained the unfiltered water or reservoir. On the Spanish islands, filters of this type were called* estelladoras.

opposite:
fig. 88. A typical colonial Dutch West Indian kitchen, painted red to hide the oven smoke stains, with painted white dots added to help reflect the light

87

English

Throughout the sixteenth century the English were constantly challenging the Spanish claim to exclusive possession of the Caribbean. During the reigns of Queen Elizabeth I of England and King Philip II of Spain, the two countries' relationship deteriorated as English buccaneers successfully plundered many of the Spanish treasure ships that carried precious cargo. In search of new lands for growing tobacco, the English settled in Saint Christopher (Saint Kitts) and Barbados in 1624 and in Nevis the following year. By the 1640s England had settlements in Antigua, Montserrat, and Saint Lucia, and in 1655, England claimed its biggest prize, Jamaica. Barbados became the first British colony to cultivate sugar on a large scale. It was not long before plantation owners could net 200 to 300 percent profit in the good years. The sugar economy made England a major economic power, as money from the islands' plantation economy was reinvested in naval strength and new plantations. On a larger scale, wealth from the West Indies funded the homeland's economic development and England grew from a northern European force to a dominant world power.

fig. 89. Rose Hall, built between 1770 and 1780, is a fine example of the late eighteenth-century Jamaican Great House.

fig. 90. *The interior of Good Hope, a Great House on Jamaica, showing nineteenth-century mahogany settees and* campeche *chairs*

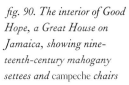

There are few records of the early seventeenth-century plantations or their functions and even fewer descriptions of the homes or furnishings. Records indicate that toward the latter part of that century, the planters began to live more luxuriously. Visitors to Barbados during the early sugar days commented on the rich dress and food of the island gentry. While there are no exact descriptions of large plantations and their furnishings, there are a few surviving household inventories from smaller plantations of approximately one hundred acres and close to a dozen laborers. These inventories, from the 1640s and 1650s, show a great change in living style from the island's earlier tobacco days, but it was still not sumptuous. The planters lived in two- or three-storied wooden houses and slept in mahogany four-poster bedsteads. Their rooms were furnished with numerous tables, chairs, benches, cushions, and carpets rather than the barrels and chests used earlier. Framed pictures hung on the walls, linen and pewter (but little or no silver) filled the cupboards, with an occasional framed mirror or clock, as well. One planter (1649) boasted a library, complete with forty-five volumes; and another (1658) had a railed balcony in his dining room and a polished marble porch floor.[33]

By the 1670s, Spain had recognized England's claims in the West Indies with the Treaty of Madrid and by the 1680s, Barbados's sugar industry was prospering and the island was considered England's richest western colony. In 1700, a French missionary priest who visited Barbados commented on the plantation houses, "One notices the opulence and good taste of the inhabitants in their magnificent furniture and slaves of which they all have considerable quantities."[34] With the exception of the North American colonies of Massachusetts and Virginia, there were more inhabitants in Barbados than in any other English colony. But by the early 1700s, absenteeism was becoming a way of life for many of the "Bajan" (i.e., from

93

opposite:
fig. 91. An English West
Indian hat stand at Bellevue
Estate, a country mansion on
Jamaica

fig. 92. The interior of Rose
Hall, with Jamaican
mahogany four-post bedstead
and Regency mahogany
chaise

fig. 93. A colonial expression
of form, a cart of courbaril
wood from the English
Windward islands. This one
is from a private collection on
Saint Lucia.

92

111

112

95

96

opposite:
  *fig. 94. The interior of a
  typical eighteenth-century
  English Great House on
  the islands*

  *fig. 95. A large early nine-
  teenth-century Jamaican
  mahogany side table*

  *fig. 96. A mid-nineteenth-
  century mahogany Bajan
  sideboard. The painting,
  a view of Saint Thomas,
  is by Camille Pissarro.*

overleaf:
  *fig. 97. A large early nine-
  teenth-century mahogany
  bedstead with palm frond
  and stylized pineapple carved
  headboard*

  *fig. 98. A nineteenth-century
  mahogany Jamaican bed
  with carved stylized palm
  frond headboard and pineapple turned post*

99

Barbados's *sugar* industry was prospering and the

100

fig. 99. *A pair of nine-teenth-century Jamaican mahogany small beds, with a night convenience chair in the background*

fig. 100. *An unusual English West Indian cour-baril wardrobe with a high, scrolled pediment top, found on Saint Lucia*

island was considered England's richest *western colony.*

fig. 101. This diagram denotes the woods incorporated into the top of the table shown below it. The woods include "mahoe" (mahogany), as well as bullet tree or bullet wood (Mimusops globosa), *fustic* (Chlorophora tinctoria), *and* ebony (Diospyros virginiana), to name a few. The diagram is inscribed, "The top of this table made in Jamaica from every wood in the island."

fig. 102. An early nineteenth-century specimen tilt-top table attributed to Ralph Turnbull. The molded circular top is composed of specimen Jamaican woods with a central compass star inlay boss surrounded by one border of interlocking chevrons and another of alternating dark and light wood pieces.

fig. 103. A detail of the table shown below

fig. 104. Jamaican specimen wood tilt-top center table, c. 1835–40, made by Ralph Turnbull in Jamaica of thirty-two indigenous tropical woods, including cashew, coconut, grapefruit, and mahogany, surrounded by a speckled bamboo border. The table is part of a larger suite that was made for Lord Sligo, Jamaica's then governor-general.

101

103

102

104

105   106   107

Barbados) planters as the other English islands of Saint Kitts, Nevis, Antigua, Montserrat, and Jamaica were just beginning to establish their own slave-based sugar plantation systems.

Many of the proprietors live in England; and those who occasionally visit their estates leave their young children behind in school. The adventurers in trade, or service on the plantation, who have resided and survived the age of fifty then return to England or Scotland with the fortunes which they may have acquired.[35]

The practice of absentee ownership had adverse effects on the islands. By spending their time in England and sending their children off-island to be educated, the planters impeded the development of school systems, hospitals, and social services. By the eighteenth century, Bajan planters had exhausted the soil and were overtaken by Jamaica as the major producer of "sweet gold."

In Jamaica, during the first half of the seventeenth century, predictably the first major structures were forts, churches, and plantation houses. Few great houses survived from the seventeenth century, but those that did resembled small English manor houses rather than the later island great houses of the eighteenth century. During the eighteenth-century colonial era, Jamaica developed an architectural style that incorporated the classical components of the English Georgian style. These features were then adapted to achieve maximum coolness for comfort in the tropical climate.

fig. 105. A specimen wood box by Ralph Turnbull

fig. 106. A Ralph Turnbull label, reading: "Manufacturer, Cabinet and Upholstery Furniture, Kingston, Jamaica."

fig. 107. Detail of a Bajan (from Barbados) mahogany and caned rocking chair, showing a carved paw foot

overleaf:
fig. 108. A particularly fine English colonial West Indian carved mahogany and caned settee found on the island of Nevis, now on Saint Lucia

fig. 109. A bedroom furnished with typical "down island Caribbean" colonial pieces made of courbaril wood, Saint Lucia

fig. 110. Two Bajan mahogany and caned armchairs, with carved paw feet

Furniture design developed concurrently with evolving architectural styles.

...the standard of comfort and elegance rose considerably. A unique description of household equipment can be found in a detailed inventory of the contents of a large house on Nevis...the house contained fine furniture of all kinds, ... A Damask bedstead...2 Elbow chairs with stuffed seats covered with silk...one Cane Couch with a Squab...a Walnut case of drawers...a black japanned tea table, a large walnut oval table...a Cane Couch and 12 Cane Chairs...a corner japanned Cupboard. John Pinney, the son of the founder of the family sugar fortune on Nevis, had probably brought this furniture with him from London where he and his wife moved in fashionable circles.[36]

The few seventeenth-century pieces that survive display simple forms with straight lines and decorative turnings. In the late seventeenth century and with the advent of the Queen Anne period in the early eighteenth century, curvilinear shapes began to prevail. Chairs with reverse-curve cabriole legs ending in pad feet and center back splats from seat to crest rail are typical of the period. The mid-eighteenth century ushered in more Georgian influences. The subsequent ascendancy of Thomas Chippendale designs that followed the Georgian style in England was not lost on the islands. As a result, cutout work lightened the chairs' previously solid back splats and the straight Marlborough leg was introduced. Finally, by the early nineteenth century, the English West Indies felt the influence of lighter, geometric Neo-Classical forms such as straight tapered legs, serpentine-shaped fronts on sideboards, and interpretations of the Greek klismos chair. The Neo-Classical style was succeeded by the heavier and more ornate Regency style of the second decade of the nineteenth century.

Generally, English colonial West Indian furniture has similarities to North American colonial furniture. Close examination, however, reveals considerable difference between the two styles. The English colonial West Indian furniture used a greater amount of wood and simpler construction methods to create the larger and bolder proportions present in even its most graceful examples. Throughout the eighteenth century, the chief source of tropical hardwoods (particularly mahogany) was the virgin forests of the West Indies. Mahogany was indigenous to Cuba, Hispaniola, and Jamaica. According to shipping records, the majority of the mahogany shipped to England came from Jamaica, but not all the mahogany shipped from Jamaica was actually cut there. As there are no records of mahogany imports from the Spanish West Indies, it is probable that the English merchants purchased Spanish mahogany from Cuba and Hispaniola and shipped it to Jamaica, where it was then shipped out with the Jamaican mahogany. An excerpt from the *History of Jamaica* (1774) verifies this idea:

> The greater part of what is shipped from the island has been imported from the Spaniards, with whom it grows in great abundance near the coast, and is cut and carried at a very trifling expence [sic], so that they can afford to sell it extremely cheap; but it is sappy, and very inferior to the Jamaica wood.[37]

The "cart," which looks like a double-shelf console, is a form of server often found in both the English and the French Lesser Antilles. In the eighteenth century, double-tiered serving tables were used in the Great-House dining rooms on the English islands, particularly Saint Kitts, Nevis, and Antigua. In the early nineteenth century, the prototype serving tables were imported from England with metal casters, which allowed for the mobility that facilitated food service. The constant humidity and salt air, however, rendered even brass casters ineffective and eventually destroyed them. When the local cabinetmakers copied the cart forms they did so without including casters, which were expensive to import and designed to fit the original imports. As a result, serving tables were still known on the English Lesser Antilles as "carts," even though they were made without wheels. This name then spread to other English islands, and to the nearby French islands of Martinique and Guadeloupe, as well.

One of the most unusual terms for a piece of West Indian furniture is the local term "wagon." Used only on the English island of Nevis, the term refers to Nevisian-made small server/sideboards. Similar in form and function to the carts found on the French islands and the cupping tables on the Danish islands, the "wagon" however had cupboard doors or drawers below the upper shelf. This Nevisian variation does not occur on other islands, and although examples have been discovered on Saint Kitts and Anguilla, these were probably imported from Nevis or made by an immigrant Nevisian furniture maker.

overleaf:
fig. 111. Two Jamaican campeche *chairs*

fig. 112. A collection of nineteenth-century West Indian courbaril wood furniture from "down island" (Saint Lucia). The caned récamier is particularly rare.

French

Although Columbus landed on what were to become the French islands of Guadeloupe and Martinique in 1502, the Spanish immediately dismissed these lands because, like all the Lesser Antilles, they held no deposits of precious metals. With the exception of French buccaneers' occasional attacks on Spanish treasure fleet vessels, the French posed little threat to the Spanish during their first hundred years of Caribbean domination. It was not until the first half of the 1600s that the French established a settlement on Saint Christopher (only to eventually lose it to the British) and laid claim to Martinique, western Hispaniola (or Saint-Domingue, as Haiti was called until its formal independence in 1804), and Guadeloupe (and its smaller surrounding islands of Marie-Galante, Les Saintes, and La Desirade), as well as Saint Barthélemy (Saint Barts) and Saint Martin/Saint Maarten (which today is half Dutch). French advances began in 1625 when the nobleman Pierre Belain

fig. 113. A typical French colonial plantation house

In response to the myriad **climatic** *demands, the French colonial Great*

d'Esnambuc led a party of one hundred settlers from Saint Kitts to Martinique, where he founded a colony. Considered to be France's main outpost in both the Lesser and Greater Antilles, Martinique soon became France's administrative center in the West Indies; and, with the exception of two short intervals when the British occupied Guadeloupe and Martinique, both islands have remained French throughout history.

Unlike other European colonists, many of the early French immigrants and settlers were of noble background and their passage was paid by the Compagnie des Isles d'Amérique (The Company of the Isles of America) established by the noblemen to administer the French dominions. As an incentive, the company offered privileges and financial aid to carpenters and woodworkers to travel to the New World. During these early years of colonization, the French produced mainly indigo and tobacco, but then followed the example of the Dutch colonies and gave precedence to sugar cane. It was not long before the French realized that the labor force of the voluntary settlers was inadequate for the labor-intensive harvest of the sugar cane crop. The French then followed the example of the other colonizing countries and began to import slaves from Western Africa.

France was connected with Spain by dynastic ties. Members of the House of Bourbon were firmly seated on the thrones of both countries, and they had long been England's chief rivals for the trade of Spanish America. France and England would continue to confront one another in the Caribbean throughout the eighteenth century. The governments of both appreciated the immense wealth of the sugar industry and also understood the importance of the slave trade. As a result, each nation was resolutely determined to monopolize the trade of its colonial islands. Their antagonism was the impetus for a series of wars that shaped the history of the sugar islands throughout the eighteenth century. The wars in which France was engaged, both at home and abroad, intermittently crippled the commerce on the productive French sugar islands. The tremendous significance of

Houses featured **verandas,** *balconies,* *and* **louvered windows.**

fig. 114. Habitation Clément, on Martinique, a typical French colonial plantation house

115

fig. 115. A French colonial Great House second-floor bedroom with a balcony and louvered French doors, showing a pair of single-door armoires

opposite:
fig. 116. French colonial homes featured porches, verandas, and louvered windows to help keep the interiors cool.

the sugar economy became abundantly evident during the diplomatic negotiations that concluded the Seven Years' War (1756–1763). Having lost to Britain, France chose to cede Canada rather than give up the sugar islands of Martinique, Guadeloupe, and Saint Lucia.

Although French colonial plantation houses were more ornate than the townhouses, they were less grand than the great houses on the other nations' Caribbean islands. There was no predominant style in colonial architecture of the French islands, either. The varied styles that emerged over the seventeenth and eighteenth centuries were drawn from various French modes, but they also reflected the tropical Caribbean lifestyle. As such, in response to the myriad climatic demands, the French colonial Great Houses featured verandas, balconies,

below:
fig. 117. A French West Indian récamier made of mahogany and hand caned

opposite:
fig. 118. A particularly fine French West Indian mahogany games table, with beautifully carved decorative motifs

louvered windows, and overhanging eaves. Continental France's Mediterranean location contributed to their adroit use of these cooling architectural features, while varied construction materials that included pink coral, volcanic pumice stone, brick, and corrugated iron contributed to their stylistic diversity. Roof dormers and hipped fish-scale tile roofs were details that were, however, exclusively French.

When mahogany was introduced to French *ébénisterie* during the middle of the eighteenth century, the wood was given the name acajou and was often referred to as such in historic documents from the island. Lafcadio Hearn's *Two Years in the French West Indies* (1890) provides an invaluable short description of Martinique's other tropical woods:

> *The courbaril, yielding a fine-grained, heavy, chocolate-coloured timber; the balata, giving a wood even heavier, denser, and darker; the acajou, producing a rich red wood, with a strong scent of cedar; the bois-de-fer; the bois d'Inde; the superb acomat,—all productiveness is eighteen times greater than that of European soil. All Martinique furniture used to be made of native woods; and the colored cabinet-makers still produce work which would probably astonish New York or London manufacturers.*[38]

below:
fig. 119. A mid-nineteenth-century French West Indian mahogany console from Habitation Clément, Martinique

opposite:
fig. 120. This serving table is early nineteenth-century and is finely designed, with a thin mahogany two-board top pinned to the frame and slender, crisply turned and tapered legs. Although found in the Danish West Indies, this mahogany side table was probably made in the French West Indies.

In Martinique, Haiti, and Guadeloupe, the furniture—unlike the architecture—displayed a decidedly French accent, but without the elaborate marquetry and gilt-bronze mounts that were popular with the Parisian *ébénistes*. The earliest forms follow the graceful free-form curves of the Baroque and Rococo styles. These evolved into the much simpler geometric Directoire style, but still retained some graceful curvilinear lines. The heavier Empire style of the Napoleonic era then became fashionable, and when the Empire period came to its conclusion, so too did French dominance in art and fashion.

French island cabinetmakers were always eager to offer the latest fashion from the mother country.

> *…the artisans who, by their culture, their ingenuity and their intelligence, were able to adapt the fashions to fit the climatic imperatives and the tropical woods… to Antilles furniture*[39]

119

When the Empire period came to its conclusion, so too did French dominance in art and fashion.

As a result, the French "Creole Style" was far more closely representative of the imported prototypes and far less interpretive than other colonial styles. With only the most subtle additions and mutations, the Creole Style was thought of as a provincial, or regional, rather than an independent style.

In France during the nineteenth century, industrialization and mass production caused furniture to lose some of its inventiveness; earlier periods' styles were reinterpreted, often distorted, and then manufactured. Throughout the nineteenth century, French revival fashions were most popular, and widely copied, particularly the Louis XV style. On the French islands, the Louis XV style spread throughout and its impact "was profound and translated locally with a number of characteristics."[40]

Armoires, which remain France's most popular furniture form, are found throughout the French islands. Most French West Indian armoires feature recessed door panels and either double- or triple-headed molded frames around the inside of these panels. The adroitly carved, curvilinear doorframes are shaped in asymmetrical patterns typical of the Louis XV Revival style. Other decorative elements common to these armoires are: scalloped skirts; short cabriole legs that terminate in scrolls resting on small pads, known as "roquillard" feet; elaborate escutcheons; and brass fiche hinges. The commonly used fiche hinge is an elongated round-headed pin-type hinge that allows the door to be removed or replaced easily. Brass double S-shape escutcheons and fiche hinges were found only on the French islands, where they were imported specifically for the purpose of stylishly finishing off the island-made armoires.

As common in the French West Indies as the four-post bedstead and the armoire was the console, often referred to as a "console Martiniquaise." These consoles were commonly used in every room in a home: bedroom, dining room, hallway, and parlor. The rectangular consoles were made of

fig. 121. A nineteenth-century mahogany console in the Louis XV Revival style

123

opposite:

fig. 122. A rare solid mahogany and mahogany veneered French West Indian settee in the Empire style

fig. 123. A console martini-quaise, *commonly used in every room of a French West Indian home: bedroom, dining room, hallway, and parlor*

fig. 124. A group of French West Indian mahogany furniture, including a caned rocking chair, a console martiniquaise, *and a caned, folding-extended-arm planter's chair*

124

126

fig. 125. *A typical example
of the mahogany beds found
on Guadeloupe and
Martinique*

fig. 126. *French West
Indian cabinetmaker
Julien Ponceau*

127

fig. 127. The bedroom of an early seventeenth-century French plantation house. The Martinician nineteenth-century bed is typical of French West Indian design.

opposite:
fig. 128. A colonial French West Indian games table from the third quarter of the nineteenth century

mahogany or courbaril. The console frieze contained either one or two drawers and the legs generally had bulbous turnings with a series of ring turnings above and below. The whole piece stood on a rectangular plinth base with ball-and-ring turned feet. The English variation of the console is sometimes mistakenly referred to as a "cart" (see fig. 93).

Another form common to the French islands and popular throughout the West Indies was the settee. The undulating, curvilinear design of the settee shows the influence of imported French furniture on the craftsmen of the French islands, especially Martinique and Guadeloupe.

A typical French West Indian daybed is the mahogany and caned récamier, often called a "méridienne," "fauteuil récamier," or "récamier sofa"(see fig. 117). These French West Indian caned récamiers are a popular regional design and, along with the planter's chair and rocking

129

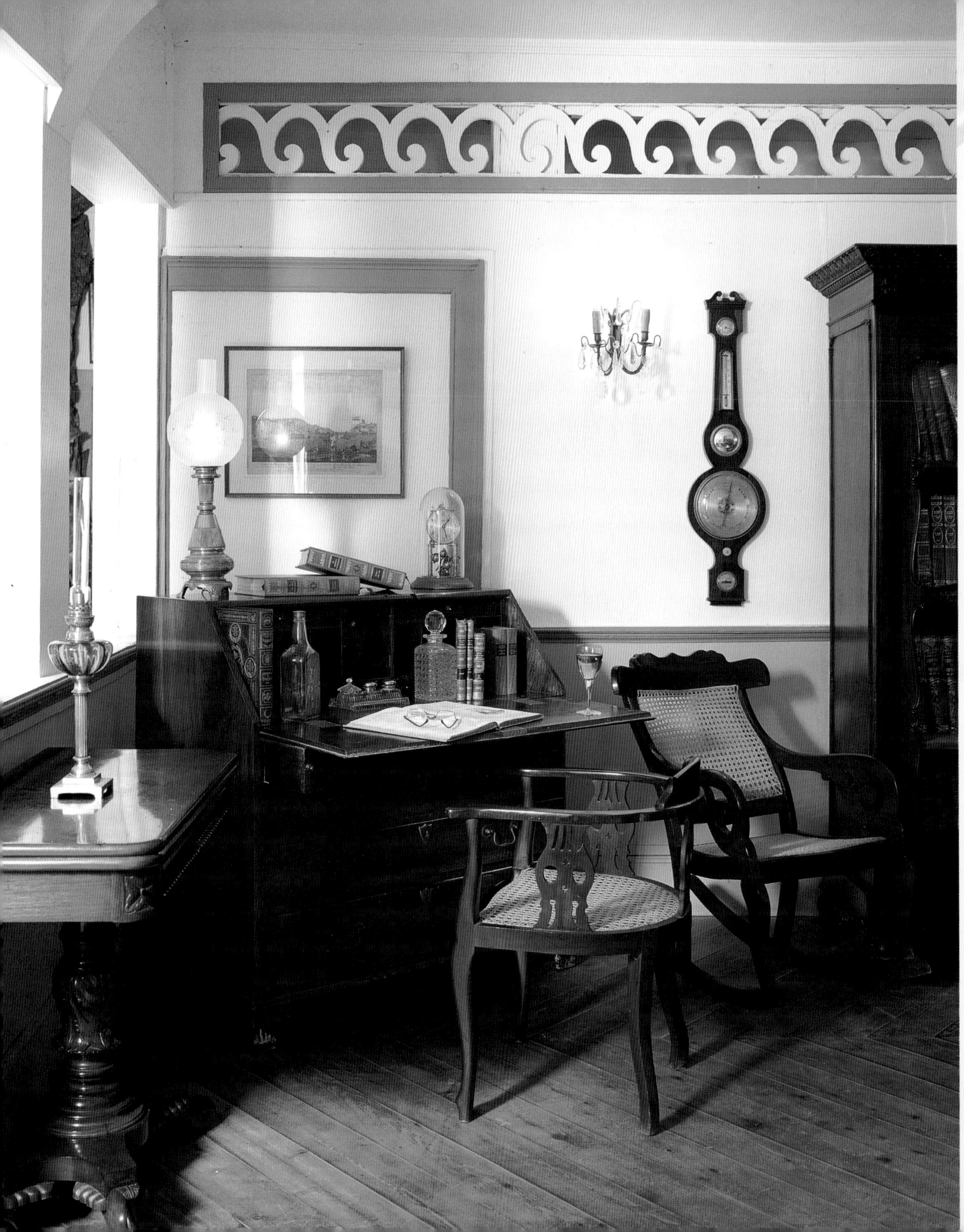

chair, are found throughout the French islands. The French island récamiers were constructed with both left-handed and right-handed backs and were sometimes commissioned in pairs.

The innovative form of the *tête-à-tête* (a conversational settee for two people) was introduced in the 1820's, a period of great prosperity. The shape of the *tête-à-tête* allows two people seated in opposite directions on the same piece of furniture to face each other and converse. The *tête-à-tête* was extremely popular and was considered the height of fashion at the time. Called "le confidant" in the French islands, the S-curved crest rail continues into low arms with curved handholds (see fig. 132). Below the crest rail are fourteen turned spindles doweled into a lower rail that terminates at and is mortise-and-tenoned into the underside of the curved arms. Between the lower back rail and

the seat are eight small ring turned spindles. Two round plain mahogany framed caned seats with rounded edges are supported on five legs. Where the two round seats meet, they share a tapering ring-and-vase turned leg and each seat has two West Indian modified cabriole legs to balance the piece. This modified cabriole-shaped leg is found not only on the French islands, but throughout the West Indies and is used for settees and chairs, as a foot form on candle stands and tables and even as hooks on hat stands.

opposite:
fig. 131. A French colonial West Indian mahogany desk. Most plantation houses had an office on the ground floor with a "compting house desk" similar to the one shown.

fig. 132. A tête-à-tête, *or* confidant, *as it is referred to in the French islands, is a conversational settee for two people.*

opposite:
fig. 133. A smaller French West Indian armoire crafted from mahogany and courbaril wood. This size armoire would be comparable to the Danish West Indian parlor press.

fig. 134. A French West Indian armoire

In times of drought, molasses was sometimes used instead of water; and to this day, the walls may seep molasses.

Danish

The manufacture of Danish West Indian furniture began around the mid-eighteenth century when King Frederick V seized control of the islands of Saint Croix, Saint Thomas, and Saint John from the Danish West India and Guinea Company, and made the three islands crown colonies. The islands, now known as the United States Virgin Islands, remained under the Danish (with the exception of a few brief intervals of British rule) throughout the colonial era until the second decade of the twentieth century (1917), when the United States purchased them from Denmark. Like many early colonies, the Danish islands began primarily as cotton, tobacco, and sugar producers. However, sugar quickly took precedence as the most important product of the islands, and by the third quarter of the eighteenth century, the Danish West Indian islands prospered from the production and exportation of sugar and its byproducts. This was especially true of Saint Croix, which had larger landmass and more fertile soil. Denmark was a relatively small country compared to the more powerful European nations, but through persistent and resourceful enterprise, the Danish colonists were able to develop one of the richest plantation agricultures.

The colonial adaptation of eighteenth-century Neo-Classical architecture was interpreted and transformed for the tropical climate and became a trademark of the Danish West Indies. Saint Croix's Christiansted architecture, most of which dates from the prosperous

eighteenth and early nineteenth centuries reflects its status as the Danish West Indian colonial capital, a status it retained from 1755 to 1871. The Danish islands' elaborate, highly classical architecture was unrivalled in the West Indies—a factor that distinguished the Danish islands as some of the wealthiest sugar islands in the Caribbean.

The architecture of the last half of the eighteenth century in Europe was based on the rediscovery of the Roman and Greek classical periods. This style reached Denmark and from there, the Neo-Classical and Greek or Classical Revival styles were exported to the West Indies.

Most buildings erected during the Danish colonial period have some degree of Neo-Classical detailing. The classical influence ranges from the design of an arch with proper proportions to the execution of a columned and pedimented entry surround.[41]

In addition to the influence of the tropical climate on design and construction, residence owners, government inspectors, surveyors, and architects frequently played an important part.

The Danish historian Jens Vibach has written that Governor-General Balthozar Frederick von Muhlenfels had exceptional merit as an architect. Vibach credits him with the restoration of Government House, Christiansted, 1800, and with the design of a number of public buildings whose drawings bear his name; he had served as chief building inspector from 1791 to 1795.

Vibach further bestows on Muhlenfels the honor of being one of the men who created the classical Danish West Indian style of building.[42]

In *Leaflets from the Danish West Indies*, Charles Taylor wrote, "…almost every estate on the island had its "Great House" where the owner and his family generally resided. Some of these dwellings were built in a most substantial manner, not a few laying claim to architectural beauty."[43]

The names of the Danish Islands' plantations—Anna's Hope, Big Diamond, Wheel of Fortune, Judith's Fancy, and Betsy's Jewel—clearly express the vanity, pride, and expectations of the new slave-owning gentry. In his book on Saint Croix, Eric Lawaetz states that at the beginning of the nineteenth century, "The estate owners could live high and as a rule they did. The buildings were furnished with much luxury. Many ate only from silver plates and drank out of crystal glasses. The furnishings were generally of very heavy mahogany and included gilt mirrors. The matadors (successful planters) gave the big lords and barons in Denmark a run for their money."[44] As on the other Caribbean islands, the planters' impressive great houses and the merchants' large townhouses were filled with fine furniture and other appurtenances of wealth.

The West Indian planters may have been demanding about the layout and appearance of their homes, but the demands they made concerning furnishing their homes on the distant tropical islands was as great. Large, handsome pieces of furniture adorned the West Indian rooms; but it was not just the furniture that gave lustre to the handsome rooms; also light fixtures, table-linen, glassware, and silver speak of the refined and cultured life the planters must have led on their large plantations.[45]

The chair from Estate La Reine on Saint Croix is a typical example of the exceptional imported Danish furniture (see fig. 140). Made of mahogany, the prominent frame and taller back differ from the earlier and lighter French-inspired Danish furniture, suggesting a date between 1830 and 1840. Undocumented provenance speculates that this chair was made for export to a government official at the Danish colony island's Government House in Christiansted. The maker has been identified only as Freund, student of the famous Danish Neo-Classical sculptor Bertel Thorvaldsen. The chair has carved sphinx arm supports, showing the Greek and Roman form of the mythical beast (a winged recumbent lion with the head and bust of a woman), and can be traced to the influence of the French cabinetmaker Jacob-Desmalter, whose name became synonymous with the Empire style during the years 1795–1814, when he was at his most influential. It was principally his furniture designs that influenced Danish furniture makers during the first half of the nineteenth century. Napoleon I was his principal patron and, as Napoleon's expeditions to Egypt brought the stylistic motifs of that country to the attention of the French, Jacob-Desmalter began to use sphinxes decoratively. It was the Greek-influenced form of the sphinx, found in Egypt only during the Ptolemaic period (323–30 B.C.), which became the model in Empire style, rather than the simpler version of earlier classical Egypt.

Danish West Indian furniture incorporates the most classical elements of all the West Indian furniture. It has strong geometric traditional lines, and often has over-scaled carving and turning. Like all Caribbean furniture, it was constructed from richly figured tropical hardwoods such as sabicu, thibet, satinwood, purpleheart, and Spanish cedar. Mahogany,

overleaf:
fig. 137. Drawing Room. Partially visible in the foreground is an eighteenth-century New York mahogany slab table that was originally part of the furnishings of Government House in Christiansted. The mahogany armchair and slant-front desk are English, c. 1800. Above the desk hangs one pair of English looking-glasses of c. 1840. The side chairs flanking the desk, the candle stand, and the window seat are early nineteenth-century Danish West Indian pieces acquired with the house. The early nineteenth-century carpet is Turkish; the nineteenth-century brass chandelier is English.

fig. 138. This eighteenth-century great house was part of the former sugar plantation named Cane Garden on Saint Croix. The south side, shown here, features a "welcoming arms" staircase typical of Danish West Indian architecture, particularly for churches and plantation Great Houses.

Danish colonists were able to develop one of the richest plantation *agricultures.*

opposite:
fig. 139. The interior of a
town house in Christiansted,
Saint Croix

however, remained the primary choice. The earliest surviving examples of Virgin Islands furniture are made of Swietenia mahogany and bulletwood (*Archras sapota*) and date from the last half of the eighteenth century.

Although most of the furniture from the Danish islands was made of mahogany, the tree was not originally indigenous; the Danes planted the mahogany trees on the islands in the early eighteenth century. Reimert Haagensen explains, in his work published in 1758, that once a planter bought his land, he would have enough wood to build all the buildings needed for the estate and be able to sell what timber was left for up to thirty times what he paid for the entire plantation.[46]

Local mahogany was not only the wood of choice of the Danish West Indian cabinetmakers, but of those in Denmark, as well. Shiploads of West Indian mahogany cut from the newly cleared Danish West Indian plantations were transported to Flensburg, the largest trading city in the duchy of Schleswig, and the most important furniture-manufacturing city in Denmark during the colonial period. In Flensburg, beautiful mahogany furniture was produced in the latest styles from the West Indian timber. Most of the furniture was eventually shipped to wealthy Danish and German households, but some pieces were exported back to the islands and sold to the affluent merchants or planters. (The recipient of the furniture is never specified on a shipping manifest; consequently, the person to whom the furniture was exported cannot be determined.)

About half of the sailing ships which in those days carried the tropical products to Denmark belonged to Aabenraa, Flensburg or Kiel. These shippers brought from

140   141   142

Denmark ham, pork, butter, cheese, and manufactured goods, which they sold in temporary booths in the West Indies. On their return, they carried sugar, rum, and other tropical products, including mahogany logs, which in Flensburg were made into furniture to be returned to the islands. Nowhere in Denmark are found as many tangible mementos of the Danish West Indies as in Flensburg. And here you will also encounter some of the same types of mahogany furniture as were common on Saint Croix.[47]

The earliest island-made furniture, whether in the form of case or seating pieces, is generally simple and plain, owing to the rudimentary skills of the first furniture makers. By the last decade of the eighteenth century, through the first quarter of the nineteenth century, imported North American and European Neo-Classical and Empire styles influenced island craftsmen to create classical forms with heavier geometric architectural design features. It is difficult to discern whether more design influences came from Europe or North America, but the distinctive style is exemplified by the Danish West Indian parlor presses and armoires, which, as previously mentioned, were preferred over chests-of-drawers. The classical architectural design of the armoire exemplifies the plain symmetrical and measured style that dominated Danish West Indian cabinet production in case pieces during the first half of the nineteenth century. Large armoires such as these were designed to be disassembled for easy transportation. They can be broken down to side panels, cornice, base, two doors, and

143

the back panels (three to six boards). This massive form was particularly popular among the plantocracy, as they owned houses large enough to contain such pieces.

> One of the freaky incidents of that hurricane was that the entire roof of McGivney Hall, immediately east of sister Jo's house in Frederiksted, blew off and smashed into the upper floor of her three-story home, and the family was obliged to go downstairs for shelter. A coachman was helping them bar up and was still working when the roof crashed into the house. They called to him to run pick up little Leslie and follow them downstairs. Perhaps he did not hear or perhaps he could not find a way down through the rubble, but he picked up the child and took him into a mahogany press to protect him from he hardly knew what. After a lull in the storm and deluge, William and Jo realized that the man had not followed instructions and come with the child. Such frantic searching and calling as began! Finally they discovered the child in the big press with the coachman, quite safe and sound and dry. This was a new use for mahogany press-es, and one that is frequently referred to within our family.[48]

Another Danish island armoire is very interesting because it is identical to an armoire in the Danish National Museum's collection as well as the armoire pictured in Tyge Hvass's *Mobler fra Dansk Vestindien*. This armoire (see fig. 146) was originally from an estate on Saint

fig. 144. An early nine-teenth-century Crucian mahogany secretary bookcase and mahogany chair with cane seat dated from the 1830s

Croix, and is now a part of a private collection on the island. It stands eight feet high and over five-and-a-half feet wide and is crafted from Swietenia mahogany and mahogany veneer. The massiveness, formality and restraint of the piece exemplify the Empire design influence. The oversized, yet subtle, classical motifs emphasize outline instead of detail and are equivalent to the Greek Revival architecture of Christiansted and Charlotte Amalie. The classical triangular pediment top has bead molding, is veneered with figured mahogany panels and fits over glue blocks that keep it in place above the flat cavetto-molded overhanging cornice. The veneered architectural frieze is incise-carved to simulate an arch curving down on the ends to meet the pilaster capital. The flat-faced pilasters are without ornament from the base to the slight indications of capitals beneath the cornice. They center a pair of veneered single panel-and-frame doors. The doors are pinned into cornice and base hardware and can be easily removed after lifting off the cornice element. The figured Swietenia mahogany veneer is laid on solid mahogany. In fact, the entire secondary construction is mahogany: the interior glue blocks; the three massive panels that form the back of the piece; and the turned mahogany escutcheons, which are original. Armoire doors are prone to splitting and warping as they are constructed of large expanses of relatively thin boards and veneer; this renders them more susceptible because of a larger degree of expansion and contraction of the wood. The interior case rails that support the removable shelves tenon into the corner stiles and are reinforced with glue. The center shelf rests on top of the medial band of three drawers. The drawers are constructed with the large and widely spaced dovetails typical of the islands and have chamfered bottoms that fit into grooves in the drawers' fronts and sides. The drawer fronts are mahogany veneered and no longer have the original pulls. The ball-and-ring turned feet are only on the front, with the back square corner stiles continuing form cornice to floor. The heavy geometric shape and bold classical forms of this armoire are the essential elements needed to date the armoire to the 1820s, but without firm documentation the attributed date could be as late as the 1830s.

The parlor press—adapted from the common armoire form—was of smaller proportions, which made it useful not only for storage but for the display of ornamental objects on top as

fig. 145. *A four-post bed-stead from Saint Thomas, c. 1845, made of Swietenia mahogany solids and veneers. The flat molded tester is supported by two mahogany head posts with convex twist turnings above a series of ring turnings and two foot posts, with two-section reverse convex twist turnings above carved, reeded sections. The bedposts end in bulbous vase-and-ring turned feet. The headboard consists of a carved stylized palm frond centered by two carved stylized zoomorphic S-curves above a row of spindled turnings. The footboard consists of a series of spindled turnings above a veneered and molded footrail. The side rails are also veneered and molded in the same manner. Each side rail has two C-scrolled and tropical foliate carved mattress blocks.*

opposite:
fig. 146. *An armoire originally from Saint Croix, identical to an armoire in the Danish National Museum's collection and to one pictured in Tyge Hvass's* Møbler fra Dansk Vestindien

162

well (see fig. 42). Danish West Indian parlor presses are similar to the clothespress form found in the southern United States after the mid-eighteenth century. The island parlor presses were often found in pairs made for the large salon areas where they held napkins, tablecloths and assorted linens. The majority of the parlor presses made before 1850 had the same Empire style as the armoires: Neo-Classical in appearance and severely geometric, with precisely balanced symmetrical elements.

Danish West Indian beds have the same substantial proportions as beds from the other islands. The earliest beds had plain tapered "pencil" posts, but by the first quarter of the nineteenth century, the beds had the typical treatment of rope-twist carving on the upper sections of the posts, and ring and flattened ball turning and stylized pineapple or

146

vase-shaped carving below. A more advanced form of the rope-twist carving was successfully accomplished by Charles McFarlane, the nineteenth century Crucian (i.e., from Saint Croix) cabinetmaker previously mentioned. McFarlane had his own shop at No. 50 King Street in Frederiksted and made coffins, built houses, and was a turner and joiner. The shop was on the ground floor and the family lived above, on the second floor. In the back, the lot on King Street extended to and adjoined the hospital. "It was a short trip from the hospital to the coffin maker's." "Attie" Petersen remembers as a child seeing a load of logs delivered on the street in front of her great-grandfather's shop. Two men who worked for McFarlane would set one log up on a tripod/triangle support and start sawing the log lengthwise into boards—right on the street. Mr. McFarlane taught the trade to his son Reginald, who became a well-known joiner and cabinetmaker in his own right. The double twist (a concave twist intertwined with the traditional convex rope-twist carving) became the McFarlanes' stylistic signature. An example of this form can be seen in the McFarlane tall-post bed shown as fig. 32.

fig. 147. A Danish West Indian mahogany bedstead that shows definitive turning with a rolling pin headboard

opposite:
fig. 148. A distinctive Danish colonial West Indian mahogany cup table with turned baluster gallery and bone inlay escutcheons

147

Records show that during this time, there were other cabinetmakers working in Frederiksted: Maxwell Plaskitt; Mr. Grant, known as Grant the Monkey Man; and Septimus MacBean, known as Seppy MacBean. These West Indian craftsmen were descendants of slaves and had learned their trade as an alternative to other, less skillful, labor.

The finely carved spindle headboards represented another opportunity for the West Indian craftsman to display the superiority of his carving and turning talents. Interestingly, the turnings on footboards were often left to shop apprentices. As a result, few of the Danish West Indian beds have sharply turned foot rail spindles; most are bobbin or spool turnings with little turning definition.

When the United States purchased *the islands, it signified the end of the colonial era and furniture* production *steeply declined.*

One of the most popular forms throughout the Danish Colonial islands is the "cup table," often called a "cupping table." The cup table was an early nineteenth-century adaptation of two separate pieces: the eighteenth-century serving table and the sideboard. Introduced during the Chippendale period, the serving table was simply a table made specifically for use in the dining area. As a furniture form, it was a forerunner of the sideboard, though it continued to be made well into the nineteenth century. The sideboard was more customized to a dining room and often included locking doors or drawers, multiple shelves, and a backboard (or splash-board) that was raised above the serving surface to protect the then-fashionable hand-painted wallpaper behind. Sideboards were introduced in Europe in 1795 but it was almost ten years later that they became popular in Denmark and another ten years after that before they became common in the Danish islands. The cup table combined the relative lightness of the serving table with the splash-board, drawers, and lower shelves of the sideboard at times, as well. Cup tables were often found in pairs or sets of four in the plantation Great House dining rooms and were light enough to be portable so that they could be used for serving on verandas and porches as well. The Danish West Indian cup table's height ranges from thirty-three to thirty-eight inches, four to nine inches higher than standard dining or serving table height. This unusual height contributed to the table's versatility by making it appropriate for use as a huntboard.

In basic form the huntboard was simply a board or frame from which a large group could be served during the festivities after the hunt. The hall or even the porch was the normal place for this activity that was so much a part of Southern tradition. The huntboard was, therefore, a serving table, and functioned in much the same way as a sideboard—but without the need for storage drawers or cabinets.[49]

fig. 149. A collection of Danish West Indian gentlemen's mahogany pieces from the mid-nineteenth century

The cup table's height, like the huntboard's, had a dual purpose: not only did it make the piece easier to serve from, but it also made it easier to eat from directly. This was convenient as the planters wore high leather riding boots, which were not well-suited for sitting down, and they would often eat standing up before heading out for the day's work.

In response to the popular revival styles of the period, island furniture makers integrated a number of the new design elements and more carving into their furniture. Their work continued to be handcrafted throughout the nineteenth century, thereby limiting the adoption of many of the machine-made revival styles. Consequently, the dominant Empire style never left island design, but was instead reinterpreted and embellished.

With the decline of the sugar economy, furniture craftsmen began to move to the Crucian towns of Christiansted, Frederiksted, and to Saint Thomas' Charlotte Amalie, where they set up shops to fulfill the needs of a new merchant middle class. The dissolution of the plantocracy had meant the end of the demand for formidable, opulent mahogany furniture. What remained was a demand for island-made furniture that resisted the climate and insects, but in simpler, less expensive forms. The growing middle class had become the primary consumers, and while they were generally aware of what had been fashionable, they had relatively small homes and less money to spend. As a result, furniture became generally less elaborate. In 1917, when the United States purchased the islands, it signified the end of the colonial era and a point at which furniture production steeply declined.

150

Conclusion

opposite:
fig. 152. This mahogany pier glass and console table are Danish, c. 1840. The mirror is believed to be one of five that hung in the ball-room of Governor General Peter Von Scholten (1784–1854), who emancipated the Danish West Indian slave population in 1848. In the pediment are bronze mounts representing the crest of Christian VIII, who ruled Denmark from 1839 to 1848.

So many of the Caribbean Great Houses stand in ruins today. As an eyewitness account of the West Indies wrote in 1871, "Most of the mansions of the planters exhibit fast-increasing signs of poverty, neglect and decay: and upon more than two-thirds of the estates the 'great house' stands deserted and empty, sometimes falling into ruin, a melancholy monument of former luxury and life, when four-in-hands were frequent upon the roads and there were sounds of revelry in the hospitable halls."[50]

There has been extensive study focused on the natural beauty, archeological excavations, colonial architecture, the history of slavery, and the socio-economic development of the islands. Very few books, however, include a study of the material culture (decorative arts) of island society. The scant bits of literature and research on the decorative arts and, more specifically, the furniture, of the West Indies lack any definitive or detailed descriptions or aesthetic valuations. As the first comprehensive account of the development of West Indian furniture and its makers during the colonial era, this book has tried to encompass a wider variety of material than has been previously considered, and presents the furniture as a decorative art form through its historical development. Although the study of the furniture of the colonial West Indies is hindered by the lack of information, it renders that study more important. It is only in the last few years that interest in colonial West Indian furniture has begun to revive. As research advances, decorative arts historians will no doubt come to appreciate more fully the far-reaching influences and contributions of the West Indian craftsmen, both freed and enslaved, to the furniture-making tradition in the West Indies and the Americas.

The West Indian furniture-making tradition may have died out, but the work of the cabinetmakers remains as a tribute to their versatility, skill, and innovative sense of design. The study of these superb pieces will continue to illuminate the creative contributions of West Indian craftsmen and their role in the social and economic history of the Caribbean islands, as well as their role in the history of decorative arts in the Americas.

Notes

1. Edward T. Joy, "Furniture of the West Indies: A Study in Eighteenth Century Trade." In *Connoisseur Yearbook, 82–88* (London Connoisseur, Ltd., 1954), 83.

2. Theodore Debooy and John T. Faris, *The Virgin Islands, Our New Possessions and the British Islands* (Philadelphia: J. B. Lippincott Company, 1918), 205.

3. Barbara W. Tuchman, *The First Salute* (New York: Ballantine Books, 1988), 15.

4. Elizabeth Rezende, "The Link to a Small German Town," *St. Thomas Daily News* (Virgin Islands), (March 26, 1992), 74.

5. Richard Pares, "Merchants and Planters." In *The Economic History Review Supplements no. 4.* (New York/London: Cambridge University Press, 1960), 38.

6. Reimert Haagensen, *Description of the Island of St. Croix in America in the West Indies,* trans. Arnold Highfield (Virgin Islands Humanities Council, St. Croix, 1995), 10; originally published as *Beskrivelse over Eylandet St. Croix I America I Vest-Indien* (Copenhagen, 1758).

7. Nancy McClelland, *Duncan Phyfe and the English Regency: 1795–1830* (New York: William R. Scott, Inc. 1939; reprint, New York: Dover, 1980), 193–195.

8. Edward T. Joy, "Furniture of the West Indies: a Study in Eighteenth Century Trade." In *Connoisseur Yearbook, 82–88* (London: Connoisseur, Ltd., 1954), 87.

9. Elbert L. Little, Jr. and Frank H. Wadworth, *Common Trees of Puerto Rico and the Virgin Islands* (New York: Viking, 1967), 251–52.

10. Tyge Hvass, *Mobler fra Dansk Vestindien* [Furniture from the Danish West Indies], trans. Nina York. Aeidre Nordisk Architektur Series, vol. IX, ed. Aage Roussell (Copenhagen: Gyldendalske Boghandel, 1947), 7.

11. Frederick Gjessing and William P. MacLean, *Historic Buildings of St. Thomas and St. John* (London: Macmillan Education Ltd.,1987),61.

12. C. G. A. Oldendorp, *History of the Mission of the Evangelical Brethren on the Caribbean Islands of St. Thomas, St. Croix and St. John* (Ann Arbor: Karoma Publishers, Inc., 1987), 225.

13. Richard S. Dunn, *Sugar and Slaves: The Rise of the Planter Class in the English West Indies, 1624–1713* (Chapel Hill: The University of North Carolina Press, 1972), 294.

14. Adolfo De Hostos, *Historia de San Juan, ciudad murada: ensayo acerca del proceso de la civilizaciaon en la ciudad espaanola de San Juan Bautista de Puerto Rico, 1521–1898,* (Puerto Rico: Instituto de Cultura Puertorriqueana, 1966), 519–21.

15. Irving B. Lyons, "Origin of the Rocking Chair: Early American Records," *Antiques,* VIII, no. 4 (April 1928): 307.

16. Ibid., 308.

17. Ibid.

18. Waldemar C. Westergaard, *The Danish West Indies Under Company Rule (1671–1754), Supplementary Chapter 1755–1917* (New York: Macmillan Co., 1917), 223.

19. Charles Edwin Taylor, *Leaflets from the Danish West Indies: Descriptives of the Social, Political, and Commercial Condition of These Islands* (London: William Dawson and Sons, 1888), 171.

20. Benno M. Forman, "The Relationship Between American and English Furniture: 1640–1840," *1981 Catalogue for the Eponymous Exhibit,* Old Lancaster (Pennsylvania) Antiques Show Committee, 43.

21. John Michael Veach, *By the Work of Their Hands: Studies in Afro-American Folklife* (Charlottesville: University Press of Virginia, 1991), 149.

22. J. H. Parry and P. M. Sherlock, *A Short History of the West Indies,* 2nd ed. (London: Macmillan,1963), 3.

23. Maria Luise Lobo Montalvo, *Havana: History and Architecture of a Romantic City* (New York: Monacelli Press, 2000), 45.

24. Llilian Llanes, *The Houses of Old Cuba* (New York: Thames & Hudson, 1999), 158.

25. Eric Williams, *From Columbus to Castro: The History of the Caribbean 1492–1969* (New York: Random House, 1984), 365.

26. Adolfo De Hostos, *Historia de San Juan, ciudad murada: ensayo acerca del proceso de la civilizaciaon en la ciudad espaanola de San Juan Bautista de Puerto Rico, 1521–1898* (Puerto Rico: Instituto de Cultura Puertorriqueana, 1966), 519–21.

27. Llilian Llanes, *The Houses of Old Cuba* (New York: Thames & Hudson, 1999), 155.

28. Ibid., 172.

29. Maria Luise Lobo Montalvo, *Havana: History and Architecture of a Romantic City* (New York: Monacelli Press, 2000), 61

30. Adolfo De Hostos, *Historia de San Juan, ciudad murada: ensayo acerca del proceso de la civilizaciaon en la ciudad espaanola de San Juan Bautista de Puerto Rico, 1521–1898* (Puerto Rico: Instituto de Cultura Puertorriqueana; 1966), 519–21.

31. Maria Luise Lobo Montalvo, *Havana: History and Architecture of a Romantic City* (New York: Monacelli Press, 2000), 121–23.

32. Barbara W. Tuchman, *The First Salute* (New York: Ballantine Books, 1988), 19.

33. Richard S. Dunn, *Sugar and Slaves: The Rise of the Planter Class in the English West Indies, 1624–1713* (Chapel Hill: The University of North Carolina Press, 1972), 76.

34. Neville Connell, "The Early Furniture of Barbados." *The Magazine Antiques* (August 1961), 459.

35. Edward T. Joy, "Furniture of the West Indies: A Study in Eighteenth Century Trade." In *Connoisseur Yearbook, 82–88* (London: Connoisseur, Ltd., 1954), 83

36. Ibid., 84

37. R. W. Symonds, "Early Imports of Mahogany for Furniture." *The Connoisseur*, vol. 94 no. 398 (October 1934), 217.

38. Lafcadio Hearn, *Two Years in the French West Indies* (New York: Interlink Books, 2001), 214.

39. Francois Darmenzin de Garlande and Joseph Poupon, *L'Art Mobilier de la Martinique aux 18e et 19e Siecles*, trans. Nancy McKinven. Department de la Martinique, office National de Forets (Paris: Hemerle, 1991), 13.

40. Roland Suvelor, *Mobilier Creole—Les Cahiers du Patrimoine*. Conseil Regional de la Martinique, N. 15/16 (July 1997), 68.

41. Betsy Bradley and Elizabeth Rezende, *Captured in Time: !919 St. Thomas, St. John, St. Croix* (St. Croix, U.S. Virgin Islands; Island Perspectives, 1987), xviii.

42. Ibid., xviii.

43. Charles Edwin Taylor, *Leaflets from the Danish West Indies: Descriptive of the Social Political, and Commercial Condition of These Islands* (London: William Dawson and Sons, 1888), 171.

44. Eric Lawaetz, *St. Croix: 500 Years Pre-Columbus to 1990* (Denmark: Paul Kristensen, 1991), 173.

45. Tyge Hvass, *Mobler fra Dansk Vestindien*, [Furniture from the Danish West Indies], trans. Nina York. Aeidre Nordisk Architektur Series, vol. IX, ed. Aage Roussell (Copenhagen: Gyldendalske Boghandel, 1947), 10.

46. Reimert Haagensen, *Description of the Island of St. Croix in America in the West Indies*, trans. Arnold Highfield (Virgin Islands Humanities Council, St. Croix, 1995), 5–6; originally published as *Beskrivelse over Eylandet St. Croix I America I Vest-Indien* (Copenhagen, 1758).

47. L. C. Helweg-Larsen, "Fra Gamle Vestindishe Hiem," [From Old West Indian Homes], trans. Nina York, *The Collector,* 1928, 113.

48. Irene Lowe Armstrong, *Cruzan Planter: Biography of Robert Skeoch* (Christiansted, St. Croix: privately printed, 1971), 76.

49. Elizabeth Bidwell Bates and Jonathan L. Fairbanks, *American Furniture: 1620 to the Present* (New York: Richard Marek Publishers, 1981), 238.

50. S. B. Hynes, "The Danish West Indies," *Harpers New Monthly Magazine* XLIV (December 1871), 198.

Index

Numbers in *italics* refer to illustrations.

Acknowledgments

An endeavor of this scope is beyond the power of one individual to complete without the assistance of a number of people. I am grateful to all friends, collectors, and scholars who were generous with their support, advice, and intelligence. Of the many people who shared resources and invaluable information I wish to thank Eusebio Leal, Historiador de la Ciudad de La Habana; Celene Valcarcel, Jefa de el Departamento de Proyectos de la Oficina de el Historiador de la Ciudad de La Habana; Llilian Llanes; Martha Castellanos Bosch, Oficina de el Conservador de la Ciudad de Trinidad; Margarita Suarez Garcia, Directora de el Museo de Arte Colonial; Robert and Sharon Bartos; Luis Coll; Jose Coleman Davis-Pagan; Luly Duke; Linda Gregory; Ena Dankmeijer; Kahrine C. G. Durguti-Martijn; Jay B. Haviser; Jacob Gelt Dekker; Mayra de Jongh; Judith Gorsira; Maurice and Valerie Facey; Tony and Sheila Hart; Norman Brick; Nancy Blackwell; Raymond Brandon; Lord Glenconner; Uta Lawaetz; Hugh Maitland-Walker; Fiona Edwards; Jeffrey and Dawn Prosser; Richard H. Jenrette; George and Cindy Tyler; St. Croix Landmarks Society; William and Susan Cissell; Barbara Hagan-Smith; David Dennis; Tony and Nancy Ayer; James and Joyce Hurd; Kai and Irene Lawaetz; Carol Wakefield; Caroline Gasperi; Annick de Lorme; Jean-Louis and Isabelle de Lucy; Betty Matthieu; Eric de Lucy de Fossarieu; Karl and Vivianne Molinard; Bernard and Catherine Hayot; Pascal and Nicole Georges-Picot; Lyne-Rose Beuze; Jean-Luc de Laguarique; Yves and Marie Hayot; and Henry Petitjean Roget.

I would especially like to thank Bruce Buck, the most talented photographer I have ever worked with, and Trudy Rosato, my business partner, whose invaluable help editing text and running the business while I worked on this manuscript made this endeavor possible. I would also like to thank Elaine Stainton, my editor at Harry Abrams, for her patience and guidance.

Lastly, I would like to record my gratitude to the people of the West Indies. I hope this study will bring a greater recognition to the furniture and furniture-makers of the islands and serve to encourage preservation and further exploration of this proud heritage of West Indian material culture.

Michael Connors

Editor: Elaine M. Stainton
Designer: Bob McKee

Library of Congress Cataloging-in-Publication Data

Connors, Michael
 Carribean elegance / by Michael Connors.
   p. cm.
 ISBN 0-8109-1009-8
 1. Furniture design—West Indies. 2. Furniture,
Colonial—West Indies. I. Title.
 NK2468 .C66 2002
 749.29729—dc21

                        2001007496

Published in 2002 by Harry N. Abrams, Incorporated, New York
All rights reserved. No part of the contents of this book may be reproduced without the written permission of the publisher.

Printed and bound in Hong Kong
10 9 8 7 6 5 4 3 2

Harry N. Abrams, Inc.
100 Fifth Avenue
New York, N.Y. 10011
www.abramsbooks.com

Abrams is a subsidiary of

LA MARTINIÈRE
G R O U P E